DOGS
OF WAR

And Stories of Other
Beasts of Battle
in the Civil War

by
Marilyn W. Seguin

BRANDEN PUBLISHING COMPANY
Boston

Library of Congress Cataloging-in-Publication Data
    Seguin, Marilyn.
        Dogs of war : and stories of other beasts of battle
in the Civil War / by Marilyn W. Seguin.
            p.   cm.
        Includes bibliographical references (.   ) and
index.
        ISBN 0-8283-2031-4 (alk. paper)

        1. United States--History--Civil War, 1861-1865.
        2. Animals--War use--History--19th century.

E468.9.S44   1998
973.7'3--dc21   97-38575
                                       CIP

BRANDEN PUBLISHING COMPANY
17 Station Street
Box 843 Station Street
Brookline Village, MA 02147

Dedication

In memory of my dachshund, Hamlet,
a heart-beat at my feet.
He doggedly remained close by
through the editorial battle
that resulted in this special book.

Table of Contents

FOREWORD 8
PREFACE 10
   Ill.: "A Little Pup" 15

Part I
COURAGEOUS CANINES:
BATTLEFIELD BRAVERY

Introduction 17
   Ill.: General Asboth and Staff at the Battle of
      Pea Ridge, Arkansas 19
Hound at Harper's Ferry 20
   Ill.: John Brown and Hostages *John Brown Harpers
      Ferry* in 1861 22
Sallie the Lion Hearted 24
   Ill.: Monument of the 11th PA Infantry
      at Gettysburg 26
Maine's Major Bites the Bullet 27
Steadfast Stonewall 28
Mascot Mike 30
   Ill.: Mike at an Army Forge 31
Jack P.O.W. 32
   Ill.: Dog Jack 34
   Battle Map of Antietam 35
The Brave Body Guard 36
   Ill.: Dog Guarding Dead Master 37
An Honorable Burial 38

The Barking Dog Regiment 39
   Ill.: Harvey 40
Loyalty Beyond the Grave 41
   Ill.: Officers and Dog Atop Lookout Mountain 43

Part II
DOG-BRAINED SCHEMES
AND OTHER PET PROJECTS:
CURIOSITIES IN CAMP AND HOSPITAL

Introduction 45
   Ill.: George Armstrong Custer and friends . . . 47
Mother Bickerdyke's Furlough 48
Mangy Messenger 50
Strange Bedfellow 52
   Ill.: Shoeing a Mule in Camp 53
A Loyal Lamb 54
Fowl Play 56
   Ill.: Lee and Traveller leaving Appomattox . . . 58
The Rat Surgeon 59
McClellan's Scapegoats 60
   Ill.: Lincoln's Dog, *Fido* 61
Camptown Races 62
   Ill.: Grand Stand Finish 65
Riding the Wooden Horse 66
   Ill.: Punishment in the Federal Camp 68
Equestrian Questionnaire 69

Part III
HAIR RAISING ADVENTURES:
SCRAPES AND ESCAPES

Introduction 71
   Ill.: Advance of the Cavalry Skirmish Line . . . 73

Sheridan's Ride 74
Sheridan's Ride by Thomas Buchanan Read 75
    Ill.: Sheridan's Ride 78
A Hare Raising Incident 79
The Mane Event 81
Morgan's Trickery 83
The Spotted Cow 85
    Ill.: Cavalry Foragers 87
Ghosts at Bull Run 88
Bird's Eye View 90
    Ill.: Old Abe 92
War Lyrics by Henry Howard Brownell 93
Stinging Encounter 94
    Ill.: A Land Flowing With Milk and Honey . . 95
The Cocky Rebel 96
Horse of a Different Color 97
    Ill.: Emma Underneath her Dead Horse 99
Clairvoyant Kitty 100
Mule Heroes 102
    Ill.: Mule Team Crossing a Stream 106
See Spot Run 107
    Ill.: Spot 109
    Prison Medal 109
    Dog Attacking Escaped Prisoner 109
Hero, the Hell Hound 110
    Ill.: Hero 112
    Castle Thunder 112
    Libby Prison 112

Part IV
GHASTLY DEATHS
AND BEASTLY BURIALS

Introduction 114

Ill.: Burning Dead Horses 116
Horse Revisited 117
Dead on His Feet 119
Ill.: Sharpshooter Improvising a Rest for
    His Rifle 121
Luck of the Draw 122
Ill.: Rebel Mules Killed by Federal Shell 124
Requiem for a Rooster 125
Sea Horse 128
Ill.: The Robert Gould Shaw/54th
    Regiment Memorial 130
Shoot to Kill 131
Ill.: Dog Tracking a Runaway Slave 133
Recipe for Rat 134
Marine Disaster 136
Old Baldy 138
Traveller's Bones 140
Ill.: General Robert E. Lee on Traveller 142
Grave Matters 144
ACKNOWLEDGMENTS 146
BOOKS CITED 148
Ill.: Dispersion of the Army
    at Shreveport, LA, May 1865 152
INDEX 153

Foreword

The Civil War was a time in which the United States found itself caught in a web of revolution. During those four tumultuous years from 1861-1865, Union and confederate armies waged a Herculean struggle for the right to determine the destiny of the country. Northern victory, however, not only confirmed that the nation was indivisible, but also obliterated the scourge of chattel slavery. Americans have been fascinated with the Civil War since Appomattox. No other event in the history of the nation has generated the publication of as many books and articles as the War Between the States.

For generations, scholars and historians have preoccupied themselves with the military aspects of America's most devastating war. A cursory review of the historiography of the war reveals a large number of studies on battles, skirmishes, generals, armies, campaigns, and regiments. The brutal nature of the great conflict manifested itself in the tens of thousands of volunteers who were killed and wounded. The literature on the Civil War is replete with examples detailing the daily life of soldiers, including heroism and cowardice, sickness and suffering, loneliness and monotony.

Marilyn Seguin has written a book generously sprinkled with anecdotal material that focuses on animals rather than men. Many soldiers carried their pets with them when they went off to war. Dogs, the most common pets, provided the recruits with both companionship and a connection to the home front. In addition to canines, other pets included cats, birds, and goats. Many military units routinely designated animals as their mascots. Old Abe, an eagle, served in that capacity for the 8th Wisconsin regiment.

Animals served many purposes during the war. Roosters were used as cock fighters to entertain the men during periods of inactivity. Both armies relied on mule power to transport baggage, often in the most inclement weather conditions imaginable. And horses were indispensable to the success of calvary units. Ironically, Traveller, the most famous mount of the war, did not belong to a cavalry leader, but rather to the legendary general, Robert E. Lee. Mules and horses endured the horrors of combat with as much courage as the troops themselves. Many of these beasts lost their lives in a cause for which they did not understand. The author maintains that "many soldiers grieved over the loss of their horses as much as they did the loss of their comrades in arms." Cattle, hogs, and chickens were some of the animals consumed by armies. As the war continued and food became scarce, snakes and rats provided sustenance for soldiers teetering on the brink of starvation.

Seguin has brilliantly described the role and significance of animals in the internal hostilities of the Civil War in her book, The Dogs of War. Analytical and very readable, this volume adds to our knowledge on the contributions of beasts to the war effort.

Leonne M. Hudson
Kent State University

PREFACE

It has never been an uncommon thing for soldiers to take their pet animals to war. In the archives of American Civil War literature, the careful reader will find many references to beloved pets, mostly dogs and horses, that accompanied soldiers into battle. However, animals of all kinds at times found their places beside the men and women who were the players of this extraordinary conflict. Some examples:

* A Minnesota regiment had a young bear which smelled powder in a dozen battles before he was sent home unharmed.

* Several Wisconsin regiments had pet badgers.

* A Confederate Arkansas regiment fought at Shiloh with their wild cat which was captured by the Federals and killed by accident.

* Another southern regiment had a pet pelican, representing the symbol on the belt of the Confederate soldiers.

* The 49th Illinois had two game cocks.

* A Wisconsin drummer had a tame squirrel that danced to martial music and spun like a top around the rim of its master's drum.

* The 12th Wisconsin regiment had a tame coon, as did the 104th Pennsylvania Infantry. Members of J.E.B. Stuart's First Virginia Cavalry kept their enormous raccoon mascot tied to a captured gun.

* The 43rd Mississippi Infantry, under Colonel William M. Moore, kept a camel named Douglas, killed by a minie ball during the seige of Vicksburg.

* The 3rd Mississippi Infantry had a 30-year-old gander that waddled along in perfect time to the music of the regimental band.

* Soldiers in one of Thomas "Stonewall" Jackson's units had a pig named Susan Jane, who was spared from the pot because the men took a liking to her.

Diaries and letters written and photographs taken during "the bloodiest of all wars" attest to the love and devotion that the combatants on both sides of the war had for their animals. More than one soldier can give credit to a horse for saving his or her life, as did Union spies Sarah Edmonds and Louis Newcome, both of whom give high tribute in their memoirs to the faithful horses that served them during the war. These animals sometimes took on larger-than-life attributes in the legends that they spawned, and several of the mascots have been immortalized in monuments that commemorate the battles in which they fought and, sometimes, died.

Not all the animals that participated in the Civil War were mascots--many of them, including most of the horses and mules, were brought along to work. The horses, of course, were used for cavalry or artillery duty. Historically, horses have been used as war animals for centuries. Before the Middle Ages, war horses were used mainly to pull light chariots manned by warriors with bows or spears, but later when firearms became the weapon of war, cavalry horses were used to carry mounted warriors. Fortunately, for the horse, though not for the warrior, modern weaponry has eclipsed the use of horses in modern-day battle (Domestic 82).

At the outbreak of hostilities in 1861, there were more than 4,500,000 horses and 450,000 mules in the states, yet before the war was over, Washington had to buy horses from Canada. Some of these animals suffered from diseases they contracted during the long, brutal marches. Hoof diseases especially plagued the horses of the army of the Potomac throughout the war. By the end of the second year of the war, a 2,650 horse hospital was operating at the Giesboro Cavalry Depot in Washington, and nearly 170,650 cavalry mounts and 12,000 artillery horses went through the hospital and rehabilitation center. Those animals that did not recover well enough to return to the field were auctioned off at $30 a head (Dawson 52).

Supply trains composed a large part of the armies on both sides, and supply wagons were pulled by hard-working mules. Mules, the offspring of donkeys and horses, are unable to reproduce. From their fathers they inherit their long ears, tufted tails and loud brays, but their impressive strength they owe, as do so many of us, to their mothers (Domestic 100). "Stubborn as a mule" can be applied to the recalcitrant nature of the beast, but nevertheless the animal was very much valued during the Civil War and relied upon to carry or pull heavy loads through adverse conditions during which they suffered along with the soldiers. During Ambrose Burnside's infamous "mud march" in January of 1863, many of the mules were so hopelessly stuck in the mud that they had to be left behind. As Colonel Robert Shaw, commander of the 2nd Massachusetts, wrote to his wife: "They [the mules] sunk so deep in some places that only their heads could be seen" (qtd. in Duncan 279). Other soldiers reported that the mules actually drowned in the mud.

Other animals were brought along to slaughter for food, as needed--usually chickens and cattle, but not always. When food became scarce, sometimes the troops were forced to eat their pack animals. When besieging Federals drew their lines tight around the Confederate troops in Port Hudson, Mississippi, the Southern quartermasters resorted to slaughtering their mules for food. Somehow, the Yankees learned of their plight and let the Southerners know it by standing on the bank one morning, braying loudly like mules. In desperate times, soldiers were forced to eat the meat of pet animals. The Confederate cook Joe Keno, for example, reportedly provided fresh dog meat in the absence of anything more suitable to sustain his troops (Davis 125).

That the men (and sometimes women) warriors formed strong bonds to the animals they took to war is unquestioned. Numerous Civil War photographs, drawings, diaries and letters, including those of Robert E. Lee, attest to the great love of man/woman for animal. And when those animals died or suffered, as they invariably did during wartime conditions, their human companions wept openly. When the war was over, a few of these animals were immortalized in monuments. At Gettysburg, for example, is the statue of a small dog curled up in sleep--or in death--a permanent memorial to the mascot of the 11th Pennsylvania Infantry (Hawthorne 32). Equestrian statuary at Gettysburg not only memorializes the horse but also symbolizes the fate of the rider. Traditionally, if all four of the horse's feet are planted on the ground, the rider made it through the battle. If one foot is off the ground, the rider was wounded. If two of the horse's feet are off the ground, the rider was killed.

This book is a collection of anecdotal material about some of the animals that served their masters and mistresses faithfully during the Civil War. Although all of the material is documented, some of the stories are admittedly legend, and the facts have probably been greatly embellished over the years. Hopefully, this small sampler of Civil War material will stand as a reminder to humans of the suffering and sacrifice of our animal friends in the brutal conflict from which our country has emerged.

"A Little Pup" (From the collection of Marcus S. McLemore).

Part I

COURAGEOUS CANINES
Battlefield Bravery

The psychological and moral comfort of a presence at once humble and understanding--this is the greatest benefit that the dog has bestowed upon man. --Percy Bysshe Shelley.

COURAGEOUS CANINES
Battlefield Bravery

Introduction

No other animal provides humans with as much loyalty and devotion as the dog, so it is no wonder that so many soldiers took along their canine companions when they went to the battlefields. Historically, dogs have fought bravely beside their human companions for centuries, perhaps accounting for the saying "to unleash the dogs of war," from whence comes the title of this book.

In 55 B.C. when Julius Caesar invaded Britain, he was startled to find huge dogs fighting courageously against his Roman legions. Sometimes these huge beasts wore coats of armor and carried mounted knives or flaming torches, and they reportedly did a splendid job of dashing among the enemy cavalry to disrupt the horses. Some of these dogs, British mastiffs, were brought back to Rome and matched against bulls, bears, lions, tigers, and even human gladiators at the Circus Maximus (Silverstein 89).

In more recent times, one famous battlefield dog was a German shepherd born in an abandoned German dugout in France in 1918 at the end of World War I. American airmen rescued the pup and his litter mates and named him after a tiny doll that French soldiers carried as a talisman during that war. After the war, the dog and his master went to California where the dog trained for shows. In his nine-year career, this German shepherd, known to the world as Rin Tin Tin, made more than forty movies and earned $1 million (Silverstein 185).

During the American Civil War, many dogs were brought along to battle as company mascots rather than as fighters, and each company thought its own dog to be uniquely gifted. Invariably these dogs formed a strong bond of love with the men and women in camp, and their performance on the battlefield often became legendary in the telling. With so many human companions, a soldier dog was sure to get plenty of attention, and if he was a good beggar as so many dogs are, he was sure to get plenty to eat. But during battle, the canine condition was "a dog's life" in the saddest sense. Many war dogs fought bravely beside their masters and were wounded or killed in the fray.

General Asboth with his dog, York, and staff at the battle of Pea Ridge, ARK. (Frank Leslie's Illustrated)

HOUND
AT HARPER'S FERRY

One of the most significant catalysts for the American Civil War took place in Harper's Ferry, Virginia (now West Virginia), in October of 1859. In his plan to free the slaves by armed force, John Brown, with a force of 18 men which included several of his own sons, took nine citizens and one dog hostage and occupied the engine house in the picturesque village that was to change hands many times during the course of the coming conflict.

One of the citizen hostages, the owner of the dog, was Colonel Lewis W. Washington, grand nephew of George Washington. The dog, Bob, had been born without a tail, and was known to be very aloof and surly, even to his master. However, on the day of Col. Washington's capture, Bob's personality changed forever.

When Washington was abducted and confined to the engine house, Bob followed, dogging his master's trail. No one, not even the charismatic John Brown, could persuade the dog to leave, and Bob stayed with his master until the hostages were released the following day after a battle between Brown's men and the local militia led by Colonel Robert E. Lee. Brown, of course, was arrested, charged, convicted and hung in December of 1859, but Bob lived for many years after the incident, much favored by his master. At his death, Bob was buried in the plantation garden (Barry 89-91).

That would appear to be the end of the tale but for one thing. Stories of the supernatural appearance of John Brown pervade Harper's Ferry to this day. Some have reported watching a man that looks exactly like John Brown walk along the street in front of the stores with a large dog at his side. When they reach the fire engine house, both vanish through the closed door. Could it be that even in death John Brown cannot persuade Bob to leave? (Roberts 88)

John Brown and Hostages, sketch by James E. Taylor. (Western Reserve Historical Society, Cleveland, Ohio)

John Brown

Harper's Ferry in 1861

SALLIE THE LION HEARTED

N apoleon wrote that when two armies are probing about, a battle can be brought on by a dogfight. Indeed, at Gettysburg, it was the skirmishers that set the pace for the hot fighting of the first day of that battle.

The battle raged fiercely in the sultry heat of July 1, 1863. At the end of the Union battle line atop Oak Ridge near the Pennsylvania hamlet of Gettysburg, a small dog took her position, barking as loudly as she could at the Confederate enemy who could not hear her above the fusillade. The dog named Sallie had been given to the 11th Pennsylvania Infantry when she was a puppy and had become a comrade-in-arms, enduring the tedious marches, the heat, cold and wet of camp life, and now, the danger of battle. Sallie was said to hate three things: rebels, democrats and women. As the battle wore on, the 11th Pennsylvania was forced to retreat across the fields, and the men lost track of Sallie in the confusion. Somewhere in those crop-filled fields, Sallie must have been separated from the retreating men from Pennsylvania, Massachusetts, New York and Maine as they fled into town, following the railroad bed to the west and passing though the area that is now Gettysburg College. Although she was tired, doggedly she kept going, searching for her friends.

Unable to find her comrades of the 11th Pennsylvania, Sallie returned to the ridge where the battle had taken place, and there she lay down among her fallen friends. Sallie stood guard over her dead and wounded friends, and when the Confederates retreated, a member of the 12th Massachusetts found her still lying among her friends, weak from lack of food, but otherwise unharmed.

Sallie was returned to the 11th Pennsylvania Infantry and served with them faithfully until February 1865, two months before the war's end. After the battle of Hatcher's Run, Virginia, Sallie was found on the battlefield, shot through the head. The men buried her on the field of battle, despite heavy fire from the enemy.

Visitors to the Gettysburg battlefield will find a statue commemorating the heroic dead of the 11th Pennsylvania as they drive through Doubleday Avenue. The soldier atop the monument faces the field, not the road, and few visitors bother to get out of their cars to examine the entire monument. If they did, they would find another statue at the front base of the 11th Pennsylvania monument, that of the small, brave dog called Sallie (Hawthorne 32; Lippy, Nesbitt 71).

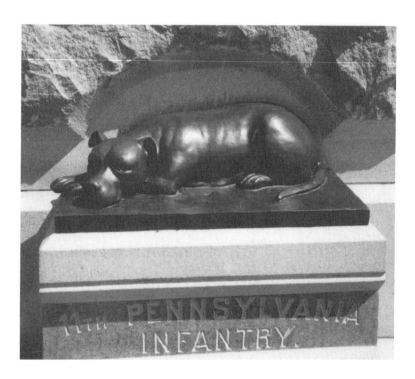

Sallie and the Monument of the 11th PA Infantry, Gettysburg, PA.
(National Park Service)

MAINE'S MAJOR
BITES THE BULLET

Soldiers during the Civil War used a new kind of bullet called the minie ball, a conical shaped projectile with grooves cut into the base that matched grooves cut into the gun barrels. When the minie ball hit something, the conical tip would flatten out causing a gaping wound, with much damage to the bones and tissue. During the Civil War, as in no other war before or since, amputation was the common medical operation for a bullet wound in any limb (Beller 27).

Most of the Civil War battle injuries, 94 percent in fact, were caused not by shells or canisters, but by bullets, mainly the new minie balls. They were deadly, as one regimental mutt found out. Major, the mongrel that accompanied the 29th Maine into battle, was said to snap at minie balls in flight as some dogs snap at flies. The game was Major's way of "having a ball" his regiment joked. When the unit was sent to Louisiana, Major accompanied the men. There, Major caught his last bullet literally, and died at Sabine Cross Roads during the Red River Campaign in 1864 (Robertson, Tenting 150).

STEADFAST STONEWALL

The Confederate artillerist rubbed the smoke out of his eyes during a lull in the fighting. When his vision cleared, he checked his limbs to make sure he was still in one piece, something he did after every battle during the fierce fighting that summer of 1862 near Richmond, Virginia. Arms, hands, legs, feet, all there. He was gazing off into the haze-filled countryside when he first noticed it, a small thing waddling out of the woods to his right, making its way to the line of cannoneers of the Richmond Howitzer Battalion. A young raccoon, he thought, probably frightened out of its tree hole by all the gunfire. But as the creature came near, he saw that it was a puppy--white, with black spots pasted on its short hair. The puppy ran right up to the surprised artillerist, who scooped up the pup and named it Stonewall Jackson, in honor of his general.

Stonewall grew and thrived in the camp with the men of the artillery. The dog became especially attached to the chief of the gun crew, Sergeant Van, who taught Stonewall the fine points of soldiering. Van taught the dog to stand at attention clenching a little pipe between its teeth. Then, just before roll call, Van took the pipe from the dog's mouth and inserted it between the toes of the dog's forepaw. During roll call, Stonewall Jackson dropped his paw to his side and stood straight and stiff at attention, eyes front, until the company was dismissed.

During battle, Stonewall dashed about wildly, barking whenever there was a lull in the shooting. But the men worried about the little dog's safety during battle, and quite often when the artillery came under fire, someone would catch the mutt and drop him into an ammunition box until danger passed. Miraculously, Stonewall was never wounded.

As canine Stonewall's reputation for intelligence and bravery spread through the Army of Northern Virginia, the little dog became the target of elaborate theft schemes, and it was a confrontation between the cannoneers and the Louisianans of Brigadier General Harry Hays that finally separated Stonewall from his beloved comrades. The Louisiana troops eventually captured the dog and hid him so well that the artillerists never found him (Abel 47-48).

MASCOT MIKE

E dwin Forbes was assigned in 1861 as staff artist
for *Frank Leslie's Illustrated Newspaper*. Forbes'
beat was the Army of the Potomac, and for two
years Forbes and his chestnut mare, Kitty, accompanied
the Army, sketching the most interesting of camp life.
Many of the 22-year-old artist's sketches included
animals, as in the accompanying drawing, *An Army
Forge*, which depicts two cavalrymen visiting a blacksmith shop to have their horses shod.

As Forbes made this sketch, his attention was cen-
tered on the trooper's scrappy little dog, Mike, who is
shown supervising the blacksmith. Reportedly, Mike
deemed himself like his owner, a cavalry scout, making
advance trips ahead of the regiment in order to gather
information on the enemy's movements.

During the battle itself, it was said that Mike loved
the boom and thunder of musket and artillery, and he
would chase after the half-spent shot, cavorting around
the battlefield like a kitten at play with a ball of yarn.
Mike was wounded twice and lost the end of his tail in
the battle at Kelly's Ford (Dawson vii, 54).

Mascot Mike at an Army Forge. Sketch by Edwin Forbes. (Dover Pictorial Archives)

JACK P.O.W.

Among the photographs that hang in the Allegheny County Soldiers and Sailors Memorial Hall in Pittsburgh, is a faded image of a black and white dog with a woebegone look that belies his battlefield bravery. However, the feisty bull terrier named Jack became legend in his own time. The most delightful version of Jack's exploits can be found in the book, *Dog Jack*, by Florence Biros.

Dog Jack raced across battlefields in Virginia and Maryland with his regiment, the volunteer firemen of Niagara, Pennsylvania. His comrades claimed that Jack understood bugle calls, and that after a battle he could be counted upon to help search out the dead and wounded of his regiment.

Jack's military career was eventful. According to a regimental historian, Jack was wounded at the battle of Malvern Hill, but recovered and was captured by the Confederates at Savage's Station. Somehow, he escaped. Jack survived the battle of Antietam on September 17, 1862, in which over 23,000 were killed, missing or wounded. It was known as the bloodiest day of the war.

Jack's luck appeared to be running out when he was severely wounded at Fredericksburg three months later, but his companions nursed him back to health. Then, at Salem Church, he was taken prisoner by the Confederates for the second time. Six months later, Jack was exchanged according to wartime protocol, Yankee prisoner traded for Confederate prisoner, at Belle Isle.

The spirited terrier rejoined his regiment and stayed with them through the Wilderness and Spotsylvania campaigns and the siege of Petersburg. Jack's regiment was so grateful for his service and companionship that they collected enough money to purchase a beautiful silver collar, worth $75, which they ceremoniously presented to their canine friend in tribute to Jack's indomitable spirit and scrappy character.

On the evening of December 23, 1864, Jack disappeared from his regiment, which was on furlough at Frederick, Maryland. His final disappearance, like his life, is also the stuff of legend, for although the men looked all over for their dog-gone mascot, Jack had simply vanished and was never seen or heard from again (Robertson, Tenting 150).

Dog "Jack."

Belonging to the 102d Reg't Pa. Vet. Vols.

Engaged in the Siege of Yorktown, the Battles of Williamsburg, Fair Oaks, Savage Station, Malvern Hill (wounded,) Antietam, Fredericksburg, Marye's Heights, Salem Heights (taken prisoner and remained six months on Belle Island, with men of his regiment,) Mine Run, Wilderness, Spottsylvania, Cold Harbor, before Petersburg, Defence of Washington, July 11, 1864; Winchester, Flint Hill, Fisher's Hill, and Middletown (was six hours a prisoner at the last battle.)

Dog Jack (From the collection of Marcus S. McLemore)

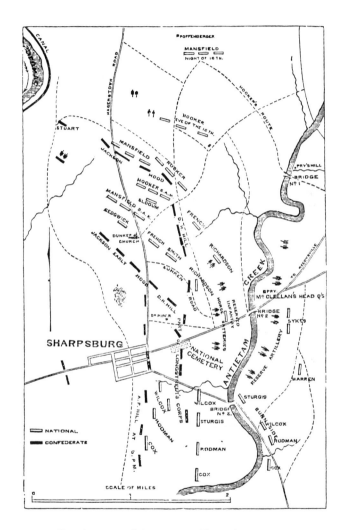

Battle map of Antietam, Sharpsburg, MD.

BRAVE BODY GUARD

On September 17, 1862, along the Antietam Creek near Sharpsburg, Maryland, McClellan finally attacked Lee's army. It was a fierce, bloody struggle and so profoundly did the reports of the fighting affect Americans, that the scene of the combat quickly became an object of civilian curiosity. Technically, Antietam was a Union victory, although strategically the battle was a draw. Both sides suffered huge losses. The Union army suffered 12,000 casualties, including 2108 killed; at least 2700 Confederates died, and 10,000 more were wounded or missing.

One of the Union combatants who fell on that awful day was Captain Werner von Bachelle of the 6th Wisconsin (another source claims von Bachelle was a member of an Ohio brigade). French born Capt. von Bachelle had brought to battle with him a faithful dog that he had trained to perform military salutes and other clever tricks. The dog fought at his side until the Captain fell, mortally wounded by a minie ball. The next morning, as the men went in to recover their dead and wounded, the little dog was found atop von Bachelle's body, dog tired but faithfully guarding his master even in death (Robertson, Tenting 151).

Dog Guarding Dead Master (Frank Leslie's Illustrated)

HONORABLE BURIAL

At the appointed time, Confederate guns east of Gettysburg opened fire against the Union enemy on Culp's Hill. When the smoke cleared, the Union soldiers could see that their return fire had repulsed the Confederates to retire out of range, leaving many of the rebel dead scattered upon the hillside. With the bodies was a small dog thought to be the mascot of the 1st Maryland (Confederate). He was limping amongst the dead on three legs as though looking for his master or perhaps seeking an explanation for the tragedy he had just witnessed.

Union Brigadier General Thomas Kane wrote of the scene: "He licked someone's hand after being perfectly riddled with bullets. Regarding him as the only Christian-minded being on either side, I ordered him to be honorably buried" (qtd. in Coco 28).

BARKING DOG REGIMENT

The 104th Ohio Infantry was known as the barking dog regiment because the men had at least three canine mascots. Colonel, Teaser, and Harvey were all veteran soldier dogs in this regiment, but the bull terrier Harvey was a special favorite. Harvey's dog tag was inscribed with the words: "I am Lieutenant D. M. Stearns dog. Whose dog are you?"

According to Marcus S. McLemore, a descendant of a member of the 104th Ohio, Harvey was wounded at least twice, once in Virginia and again in the Battle of Franklin in central Tennessee. During the latter engagement, Confederate General John Bell Hood with a force of 27,000 troops attacked the Union army of 28,000. The battle, which lasted nine hours and resulted in 6500 Confederate casualites and 2326 Union casualties, was indecisive. Harvey recovered from his wound.

Off the battlefield, Harvey apparently had an ear for music. The men said that the dog swayed from side to side when they sang campfire songs. At one time, Harvey proudly posed with the regimental band as shown in a photograph in the collection of the Western Reserve Historical Society in Cleveland.

After the war, the men of the 104th had Harvey's portrait painted for display at reunions, and Harvey's image was also incorporated into keepsake buttons (McLemore).

Harvey (From the collection of Marcus S. McLemore)

LOYALTY
BEYOND THE GRAVE

Mrs. Pfieff, like many other widows of Union soldiers killed in the battle of Shiloh, had travelled all the way from Chicago to Tennessee to find her dear husband's dead body and take it back home. Travel was hard in 1862, especially for a lady travelling alone, but Mrs. Pfieff was determined that her husband's remains be returned to his home for reburial.

When she arrived at the battlefield, she searched tirelessly among the markers of the thousands of hastily dug graves of the Union troops that had died during the two days of fierce fighting on April 6 and 7. Casualties numbered 10,000 on each side, she had been told, but she only cared about one--the casualty of Lieutenant Louis Pfieff of the 3rd Illinois Infantry.

At the end of the day, Mrs. Pfieff was about to give up--no one had been able to direct her to the grave of her husband. Discouraged and grief stricken, the widow looked up from the burial field and saw a large dog coming toward her. As the beast approached, Mrs. Pfieff recognized her own dog, one that her husband had taken with him when he had left Illinois. The dog seemed pleased to see her and she knelt and hugged the animal, burying her face in the animal's coarse fur. When at last Mrs. Pfieff stood, the dog began to move away from her, looking back at her from time to time, beseeching her to follow. The dog led the widow to a distant part of the burial field and stopped before a single unmarked grave that stood apart from the others. Trusting the dog to lead her to her husband, Mrs. Pfieff requested that the grave be opened. Sure enough, the grave contained the remains of Lt. Pfieff.

Later, the widow learned that the dog had been by Pfieff's side when he was shot, and had remained at his master's burial site for 12 days, only leaving his post long enough to get food and drink (Abel 51, 53).

Officers and dog at Lookout Mt., Tennessee (From the collection of Marcus S. McLemore)

Part II

Dog-Brained Schemes and Other Pet Projects
Curiosities in Camp and Hospital

May-be the things I perceive,
                    the animals, plants, men, hills,
      shining and flowing waters,
The skies of day and night, colors, densities, forms,
      may-be these are (as doubtless they are) only
                                    apparitions,
      and the real something has yet to be known,
(How often they dart out of themselves as if to confound
                              and mock me!)
                              --Walt Whitman

DOG-BRAINED SCHEMES AND OTHER PET PROJECTS
Curiosities in Camp and Hospital

INTRODUCTION

Not all the pets that soldiers brought to war went with them on the battlefield. Most Civil War pets were left behind in the safety of camp when the soldiers were actively fighting, but their exploits still became legendary within their regiments and the companionship of these animals helped Civil War soldiers cope with the demands and deprivations of army camp life.

When photographers visited the army camps, it was not unusual for the men to pose with the camp mascot, usually a dog. George Armstrong Custer had such a photograph taken in 1862 as he reclined outside his tent with the camp mongrel curled up on a blanket next to him (Abel 46). Civil War archives contain an abundance of photographs, etchings and journal entries that attest to the importance of animals--pets, livestock, and even vermin--in the everyday life of the soldier when he was not engaged in combat.

First Lieutenant George Armstrong Custer (reclining) and dog with members of the Federal provost marshal's staff at Cumberland Landing. (Library of Congress)

MOTHER BICKERDYKE'S FURLOUGH

Mary A. Bickerdyke, called Mother Bickerdyke by her soldier patients, was put in charge of the Union's Main Hospital at Corinth, Mississippi, in the spring of 1862, and of the Gayoso Hospital in Memphis a year later. In "enemy country" fresh supplies were often hard to come by, and Mother B's resources were taxed in order to provide for her patients. Then she hit upon a plan, and when the medical director came into her hospital one day, she confronted him.

"Doctor, do you know we are paying these Memphis secesh fifty cents for every quart of milk we use? And do you know it's such poor stuff--two thirds chalk and water--that if you should pour it into the trough of a respectable pig at home, he would turn up his nose and run off, squealing in disgust?"

"Well, what can we do about it?" asked the doctor.

"If you'll give me thirty days' furlough and transportation, I'll go home, and get all the milk and eggs that the Memphis hospitals can use," she replied.

"Get milk and eggs! Why, you could not bring them down here even if the North would give you all it has. A barrel of eggs would spoil in this warm weather before it could reach us. And how on earth could you bring milk?" asked the doctor, incredulous at her suggestion.

"Give me furlough and transportation, and let me try it!" Mother B. persisted.

And so the medical director granted the furlough, and Mother Bickerdyke traveled north to St. Louis, accompanied by several hundred war amputees. These men she had placed in hospitals, and then she continued on to Chicago where she petitioned a wealthy farmer to donate a hundred cows to her cause. Within a week, Mother B. also received many hens which were temporarily cooped up in the rooms of the Commission in Chicago, awaiting shipment to Memphis.

Before her furlough ended, Mother Bickerdyke returned to her hospital in Memphis, forming a part of a long procession that included the hundred cows and one thousand hens. Amidst the din of lowing and cackling, Mother B. told the amazed Memphians that these were "loyal cows and hens; none of your miserable trash that give chalk and water for milk, and lay loud-smelling eggs" (Botkin 140-143). Like any mother, Mrs. Bickerdyke had done gone the distance for "her boys."

Mother Bickerdyke was the only woman William Sherman would allow at the front. When Sherman's army marched in the Grand Review in 1865, Mother B. rode at the head of the Fifteenth Corps.

MANGY MESSENGER

G eneral, Mrs. M is outside to see you. She says she has the information you requested," reported the soldier posted outside the commander's tent.

"Send her in," said the General.

The tent flap opened and the beautiful and clever Confederate spy known only as Mrs. M. stepped inside. Behind her followed her pet dog attached to a leash held tightly by Mrs. M.

General Beauregard greeted Mrs. M warmly. She had been useful in supplying him with much needed information about the Union positions and movements. Then Beauregard stooped down, mostly out of courtesy to the dog's owner rather than out of affection for the dog, and gave the pooch a pat on the back. The animal's fur was coarse and springy, and the fat little dog wagged its tail in gratitude at the General's touch.

"I have the report with me, but it was hard to get it through the Union lines. Once I was stopped and they searched me thoroughly," said Mrs. M. She was feeling quite pleased with herself this evening. The General could imagine that the feisty Mrs. M. would not easily submit to having herself and her things searched.

"General, can I borrow your knife?" she asked. He handed the weapon to her, and was horrified when the woman stooped over her little pet and plunged the knife into the dog's side. He watched in horrified disbelief, but the dog was still wagging its tail, gazing with love into its mistress's face as Mrs. M. sawed away at the fake fur skin she had sewn around the dog's middle.

Mrs. M handed General Beauregard the report that she had hidden underneath the dog's second coat of fur. "I'm not the only spy with a thick hide, General," said the clever Mrs. M. (Colman 19).

STRANGE BEDFELLOW

Donkey Jason had already experienced plenty of adventure before he went to the Civil War in 1861. Jason's owner, the French army veteran Monsieur Chillon, acquired Jason when Chillon emigrated to California. Jason and Chillon together walked cross country through Indian territory in order to enlist, and were welcomed by the 3rd Louisiana of the Confederate Army.

On the first night in camp when it was time to turn in, Jason followed the regimental commander into his tent and snuggled up close, causing a good deal of hilarity among the soldiers in the camp. Jason and Chillon, you see, were accustomed to sleeping together when they traveled, and the regiment's commander looked a lot like Chillon (Davis 136).

Shoeing a Mule in Camp, sketch by Edwin Forbes. (Frank Leslie's Illustrated)

A LOYAL LAMB

Lacking a company mascot, Captain Elisha Hunt Rhodes of the 2nd Rhode Island Volunteers, adopted a young lamb from a flock of sheep brought back by a foraging party near Clifton, Va. Rhodes, whose diary and letters were excerpted on the PBS TV series The Civil War, wrote on September 18, 1864: "I selected one lamb from our flock and we are to make a pet of it. We have named him 'Dick' and he is already a great favorite" (Rhodes 174).

The next day, Rhodes received marching orders and proceeded to Winchester where he fought in the battle of Opequon. Rhodes noted in his diary on October 11 that "My pet lamb 'Dick' survived the battle and is well known in the city. He follows me or my horse wherever I go" (Rhodes 183).

The next mention of Dick is in the entry for October 25: "My sheep 'Dick' is a character and has been taught many tricks by the men. He is belligerent in his disposition, and woe be to any who is not on his guard when Dick approaches. I think I shall send him to Barnum as a curiosity in the sheep line" (Rhodes 186).

By November 1, Rhodes had moved with the 2nd R.I. Volunteers and Dick to Middletown, Va. It was here that he celebrated the re-election of President Lincoln on November 10. Rhodes wrote: "...our sheep 'Dick' took his place in line with the officers when they came up to salute at dress parade and marched with them. It made lots of fun for the boys" (Rhodes 188).

A few weeks later, Rhodes wrote about Dick for the last time. "U.S. Transport City of Albany, James River, Va., Dec. 4/64--About midnight Wednesday Nov. 30th orders came for us to move at daylight Dec. 1st. We (that is our Corps) took cars and reached Washington about noon Dec. 2nd. We took our pet sheep with us, but on reaching Washington, the field and staff officers found themselves without money, so we sacrificed our sentiment and sold poor Dick to a butcher for $5.00 and invested the proceeds of the sale in bread and Bologna sausage" (Rhodes 191).

FOWL PLAY

The Confederate General Robert E. Lee was a great lover of animals of all kinds. At one time during his U.S. Army days, Lee was crossing the narrows between Fort Hamilton and Staten Island, New York, when he spotted a dog swimming with its head barely above the water. Lee rescued the dog, took her home and named her Dart. One of Dart's pups, Spec, once jumped out of a high window in order to follow the Lee family to church. After that, Lee always permitted Spec to go to church whenever he wished (Garrison, Curiosities 81).

At the height of the Civil War, Lee kept a pet hen which reportedly laid an egg under his cot every day. The hen accompanied Lee to Gettysburg, a battle that ended disastrously for the Confederates, and when Lee began his retreat from that field, his men were unable to locate the hen. Although Lee was greatly despondent over the battle, reportedly taking the blame for the Confederate defeat upon himself, he nevertheless joined in the search for his pet hen. Eventually, the hen was found and she retreated in Lee's headquarters wagon (Davis, 206).

Lee also had a particular fondness for his war horses. Though not as well known as the famed Traveller, another of Lee's mounts was the sorrel mare, Lucy Long, a gift from J. E. B. Stuart in 1862. Never one to look a gift horse in the mouth, Lee used Lucy Long alternately with Traveller, and both these mounts outlived the General who died in 1870.

Other animals shared Lee's love, including a milk cow, who Lee said "stands next in my affections to Traveller" (qtd. in Freeman, vol 4, 309). Lee claimed that his cow was as effective as the barn cats in controlling the pesky rodent population.

Near the end of his life, Lee asked for a dog as his animal companion, "to play the part of a friend and protector." Lee was not particular about breed, but he demanded the same loyalty from a dog that he had enjoyed from his mounts. Writing a month before he died, Lee requested that the canine "not to be too old to contract a friendship for me--neither is his size so important to me as a perfect form" (qtd. in Freeman, vol 4, 310).

Lee and Traveller Leaving Appomattox

THE RAT SURGEON

Lice, rats and other pests plagued the army hospitals and prison camps of both sides. According to nurse Phoebe Yates Pember, the rats were the worst: "Other vermin, the change of seasons would rid us of, but the coldest day in winter, and the hottest in summer, made no apparent difference in their [the rats'] vivacious strategy" (qtd. in Botkin 147).

According to Pember, the patients related fantastic rat stories, saying that during the night the rodents ate all the poultices applied to their wounds. Some patients complained that the rats dragged away the pads stuffed with bran from under their wounded limbs. Reportedly, one rat even performed a surgical operation which would have entitled it to pass the medical board. A Virginian by the name of Patterson had been wounded in the instep of his left foot. The wound was terribly infected, but the doctors feared to operate to remove the infected mass because lockjaw might ensue. One morning, quite inexplicably, Patterson's wound appeared to be healing quite well, the infected mass gone. According to Patterson, some skillful rat surgeon had performed the service during the night (Botkin 148).

McCLELLAN'S SCAPE GOATS

It took only the sight of the handsome General George B. McClellan dashing along the lines astride his horse Daniel Webster to instill confidence and courage in the Army of the Potomac. McClellan shouted and waved his hat, encouraging their cheers, firing them with spirit. Oh how his men loved him!

Unfortunately for the General, President Lincoln did not feel the same away about McClellan as did the army. Lincoln repeatedly questioned the movements, or lack thereof, of the cautious and conservative McClellan. In early October of 1862, the disgusted Lincoln sent the following message to McClellan: "The President directs that you cross the Potomac and give battle to the enemy or drive him south. Your army must move now while the roads are good."

McClellan again stalled, this time blaming among other things the poor condition of his cavalry horses. Lincoln wired back sarcastically: "I have just read your dispatch about sore-tongued and fatigued horses. Will you pardon me for asking what the horses of your army have done since the battle of Antietam that fatigues anything?"

One month later the President relieved McClellan of his command, the military equivalent of changing horses in midstream. Another man was to lead the great army briefly--very briefly. His name was Ambrose Burnside (Bailey 161, 164).

Lincoln's dog, Fido, photographed in Springfield, Illinois. Reportedly, Lincoln gave this dog to a neighbor after Lincoln was elected
President. Fido never lived in the White House. (From the collection of Marcus S. McLemore)

CAMPTOWN RACES

Days in camp could be tedious for the men. Invariably they turned to games and sport to ease the boredom between marches and battles. A favorite sport was cock fighting in which roosters usually fought to the death, but in the absence of cocks, the boys would make use of more plentiful critters and race lice. According to Private Sam R. Watkins' account:

> Pharoah's people, when they were resisting old Moses, never enjoyed the curse of lice more than we did. The boys would frequently have a louse race. There was one fellow who was winning all the money; his lice would run quicker and crawl faster than anybody's lice. We could not understand it. If some fellow happened to catch a fierce-looking louse, he would call on Dornin for a race. Dornin would come and always win the stake. The lice were placed in plates--this was the race course--and the first that crawled off was the winner. At last we found out D.'s trick; he always heated his plate. (Watkins 76)

As soldiers grew weary of waiting for battle, they often challenged each other to horse races. Just a few hours before the battle of Antietam began, a pair of fools from the staff of Brigadier General Thomas Meagher's Irish Brigade chased each other into enemy territory. Surgeon Francis Reynolds and Captain Jack

Gosson went galloping off on a cross country race that took them beyond the Federal skirmish line, ignoring orders to stop. The Confederate pickets watched the race and were apparently amused enough not to shoot. Instead, the pickets shouted their approval and tossed their hats into the air (Bailey 63).

After Antietam, Lincoln removed George McClellan from command and replaced him with Ambrose Burnside on November 5, 1862. The political significance was not lost on the rank and file of the 2nd Massachusetts, who were planning a grand Thanksgiving feast followed by entertainment in the form of a horse race. They named the two horses chosen for the race "Burnside" and "Little Mac." Col. Robert Gould Shaw described the anticipated event in a letter to his sister:

> The horses will be led out heavily blanketed (which will astonish them, as I don't believe either ever heard of a blanket before) by the grooms... The two Gentlemen Riders will then arrive on the ground in a wagon--where after taking off 5 or 6 overcoats a piece they will mount & take a preliminary gallop. Capt Russell will then give the word to start & if neither tumbles off, their horses may be able to bear them three quarters of the way, when they will probably dismount & run the rest on foot." (qtd. in Duncan 260)

Shaw never says which horse won the Thanksgiving race, but a few weeks later he had the opportunity to participate in a race of his own. On Dec. 1, Shaw described the contest in a letter to his mother: "I got myself up in the foxiest possible jockey style; was beaten very badly in two straight one-mile heats, and had my pretty clothes all covered with mud, from my collar down, besides getting my hair, eyes, nose, and mouth full of the same article, from the heels of the winning horse" (qtd. in Duncan 265-6). Apparently the experience changed his mind about the sport in general, for in a p.s. to the same letter, he wrote, "I am disgusted with horse-racing, and think it is a very immoral practice, as well as ruinous to fine clothes (266)."

Besides being "immoral," racing sports could be deadly dangerous to horse and rider. Elisha Hunt Rhodes recorded one such incident in his Civil War diary:

> Before Petersburg, Va., March 17th Friday, St. Patrick's Day--We attended the celebration at the camp of the Irish Brigade (so called). The sports were rough, and after seeing one Colonel and two enlisted men thrown from their horses and injured so that they will probably die, I returned to camp satisfied the Irish celebrations are dangerous amusements. Hurdle races and ditch jumping were the principal features of the games. I like a good horse and a good run, but such sport is not to my liking. (Rhodes 211-12)

Grand Stand Finish (Frank Leslie's Illustrated)

RIDING
THE WOODEN HORSE

By the spring of 1863, the Army of the Potomac had suffered a series of serious defeats, culminating in a humiliating retreat for the Federals after Chancellorsville. As a result, the northern troops suffered from low morale, and minor offenses among the men in camp increased. Regimental commanders resorted to a number of humiliating punishments for such crimes as cowardice, drunkenness and insubordination. For the charge of cowardice, a soldier was stripped of uniform and escorted out of camp as a drum and fife corps followed behind, a practice known to the Union Army as "drumming out of camp" (McCutcheon 229).

Other penalties included having to wear a barrel shirt, dragging a ball and chain, and a painful punishment called bucking and gagging. One soldier described witnessing the latter punishment: "A bayonette or piece of wood was placed in his mouth and a string tied behind his ears kept it in position... the man was seated on the ground with his knees drawn up to his body. A piece of wood is run through his legs, and placing his arms under the stick on each side of his knees, his hands are then tied in front, and he is as secure as a trapped rat" (qtd. in Robertson, Civil 27).

In the Confederate Army, punishments were equally humiliating for the offenders. When the 27th Mississippi Infantry officers caught their soldiers stealing pigs, the officers decided to go "whole hog" on punishing the thieves. Because lack of time and facilities would not permit scalding and scraping, the thieves had skinned their victims. (A piece of skinned pork was a telltale sign of pillage.) The officers cut holes in pieces of the discarded pork skin and slipped them over the heads of the offenders who were ordered to wear the hog skin cravats all day in front of the provost guard (Wiley, Reb 233).

Another humiliating punishment was "riding the wooden horse," a practice which required the criminal to sit for hours astride an oversized wooden horse situated in the middle of camp where the rider would be met with jeers from his comrades. In one case, a deserter was ordered by the court:

> He is likewise to ride astride a wooded horse for fifteen days two hours and a half each day, the riding to be done every day in the week except Saturdays and Sundays, the horse to be six feet high, the pole upon which he is to sit to be six inches in diameter... he to go through this exercise from two o'clock P.M. until half past four P.M. (qtd. in Wiley, Reb 227)

Punishment in the Federal camp. Drawing by Peter F. Copeland.
(Dover Pictorial Archives)

EQUESTRIAN QUESTIONNAIRE

Many Civil War officers and their horses were inseparable in life. See how many matches between officer and horse you can make from the lists below. Correct matches are given at the bottom of the page.

Officer
1. *John Buford*
2. *Joshua Chamberlain*
3. *George Armstrong Custer*
4. *John Gibbon*
5. *John B. Hood*
6. *Fitz Hugh Lee*
7. *Robert E. Lee*
8. *James Longstreet*
9. *George G. Meade*
10. *J.E.B. Stuart*

Horse
A. *Charlamayne*
B. *Lucy Long*
C. *Don Juan*
D. *Jeff Davis*
E. *Old Baldy*
F. *My Maryland*
G. *Grey Eagle*
H. *Fanny*
I. *Hero*
J. *Nellie Gray*

(Answers: 1-G, 2-A, 3-C, 4-H, 5-D, 6-J, 7-B, 8-I, 9-E, 10-F. Information from Magner 46.)

Part III:

HAIR RAISING
ADVENTURES
Scrapes and Escapes

With foam and with dust the black charger was gray;
By the flash of his eye, and his nostril's play,
He seemed to the whole great army to say, "I have
brought you Sheridan all the way From Winchester
down, to save the day!"

--Thomas Buchanan Read

HAIR-RAISING ADVENTURES
Scrapes and Escapes

Introduction

I t was the impelling spirit of adventure that drew many to enlist for duty during the Civil War. Invariably, the animals the enlisted brought with them became part of the human adventure and were sometimes responsible for the greater achievements of the men and women they accompanied on and off the battlefield.

After the war finally finished, some of the animals that accompanied their owners to war were memorialized in poetry, paintings and statues. Other animal associations were preserved as images in commemorative medals and photographs taken after the war. Many, many other tributes exist in poetry and song and in the diaries and letters of the soldiers themselves. Not all of these associations were positive, however, as evidenced by the powerful hatred for the guard dogs expressed by the prisoners of Andersonville.

The anecdotes included in this section are bound together by the theme of adventure and escape--sometimes for the animal, sometimes for the human, sometimes for both--and often, for neither.

The Advance of the Cavalry Skirmish Line. Sketch by Edwin Forbes. (Dover Pictorial Archives)

SHERIDAN'S RIDE

When Confederate General Jubal Early attacked Phil Sheridan's camp at Cedar Creek, the commander himself was in Winchester, 20 miles from the fighting. On getting word of the battle in progress, the 5-foot 4-inch Sheridan leapt upon his horse (named Rienzi for the Mississippi town in which the steed had been captured) and rode hard to Cedar Creek, just in time to repulse the attack. Sheridan wrote to Grant: "Disaster has been converted into splendid victory."

Sheridan was rewarded with a promotion to the rank of major general in the regular army, but it was the poet Thomas Buchanan Read who immortalized the real hero of that day, Sheridan's horse. Read wrote an ode to "Sheridan's Ride" that became the gospel of Lincoln's re-election campaign in 1864 as the poem was read at most of the public gatherings that preceded the November election. Clearly, the poem gives most of the credit to the horse, rather than to its master Phil Sheridan, who said when asked about the famous ode: "The thing they seem to like best about it is the horse" (Lewis 292-293).

SHERIDAN'S RIDE
September 19, 1864

Up from the South at break of day,
Bringing to Winchester fresh dismay,
The affrighted air with a shudder bore,
Like a herald in haste, to the chieftain's door,
The terrible grumble and rumble and roar,
Telling the battle was on once more,
And Sheridan twenty miles away.

And wider still those billows of war
Thundered along the horizon's bar;
And louder yet into Winchester rolled
The roar of that red sea uncontrolled,
Making the blood of the listener cold
As he thought of the stakes in that fiery fray,
With Sheridan twenty miles away.

But there is a road from Winchester town,
A good broad highway, leading down;
And there, through the flash of the morning light,
A steed as black as the steeds of night
Was seen to pass as with eagle flight.
As if he knew the terrible need,
He stretched away with the utmost speed;
Hills rose and fell,--but his heart was gay,
With Sheridan fifteen miles away.

76 -- <u>Marilyn W. Seguin</u>

Still spring from those swift hoofs, thundering South,
The dust, like smoke from the cannon's mouth;
Or the trail of a comet, sweeping faster and faster,
foreboding to traitors the doom of disaster.
The heart of the steed and the heart of the master
Were beating, like prisoners assaulting their walls,
Impatient to be where the battle-field calls;
Every nerve of the charger was strained to full play,
With Sheridan only ten miles away.

Under his spurning feet, the road
Like an arrowy Alpine river flowed,
And the landscape sped away behind,
Like an ocean flying before the wind;
And the steed, like a bark fed with furnace ire,
Swept on, with his wild eyes full of fire;
But, lo! he is nearing his heart's desire,
He is snuffing the smoke of the roaring fray,
With Sheridan only five miles away.

The first that the General saw were the groups
Of stragglers, and then the retreating troops;
What was done,--what to do,--a glance told him both,
And, striking his spurs with a terrible oath,
He dashed down the line mid a storm of huzzas,
And the wave of retreat checked its course there, because
The sight of the master compelled it to pause.
With foam and with dust the black charger was gray;
By the flash of his eye, and his nostril's play,
He seemed to the whole great army to say, "I have
brought you Sheridan all the way
From Winchester down, to save the day!"

Hurrah, hurrah for Sheridan!
Hurrah, hurrah, for horse and man!
And when their statues are placed on high,
Under the dome of the Union sky,--
The American soldier's Temple of Fame,--
There with the glorious General's name
Be it said in letters both bold and bright:
"Here is the steed that saved the day
By carrying Sheridan into the fight,
From Winchester, --twenty miles away!"

--Thomas Buchanan Read

Sheridan's Ride, sketched by Civil War illustrator James E. Taylor. (Western Reserve Historical Society, Cleveland, Ohio)

A HARE RAISING
INCIDENT

At Malvern Hill on July 1, 1862, through a wide gap made in the Confederate lines by McClellan's artillery, there ran a panic-stricken bunny, flying in terror to the rear. One soldier, impressed with the rabbit's good sense, cried, "Go to it Molly Cottontail! I wish I could go with you!"

Meanwhile, Zebulon Vance's brigade of North Carolinians was lying down in line before the final advance when the scared hare sprang from the bushes, running along the ground in their front. Vance called out, "Run, little cottontail! I'd run too if I wasn't Governor of North Carolina!" (qtd. in Botkin 95-96).

Isaac W. Scherich, in unpublished memoirs penned after the end of the war, remembered a similar incident-- or perhaps the following is a variation of the same incident just described:

> Somewhere out in Virginia, we were on the skirmish line, dismounted, going through a thick piece of timber, and came to a field about three hundred yards across and timber on the other side. We had not seen anything of the enemy until we come to the field, and there they were, apparently as thick as swarming bees in the edge of that timber.
>
> Concealing ourselves as best we could behind the trees, began to shoot and of course the Rebs

were returning the compliment. The noise scared
up a rabbit from its nest in the long grass and it
went jumping at a rapid rate parallel to and mid-
way between the two lines. Johnnie, our little
Irishman, sprang from behind his tree, swung his
hat over his head and yelled "Be jabbers, go it
cotton tail. If I had no more reputation to sustain
than you have, I would run too." Our line gave
him a real Yankee cheer, which made the Rebs
swarm out thinking that we were starting to
charge on them. (63)

Rabbits may have been especially sensitive to the
mayhem of the battlefield. At Murfreesboro, a flock of
sparrows from the cedar thickets "fluttered and circled
above the field in a state of utter bewilderment, and
scores of rabbits fled for protection to our men lying
down in line of the left, nestling under their coats and
creeping under their legs in a state of utter distraction.
They hopped over the fields like toads, and as perfectly
tamed by fright as household pets" (qtd. in Wiley, Yank,
80).

THE MANE EVENT

Southern-born Union spy Elizabeth Van Lew enjoyed the high social standing of her family in Richmond, where she was always keeping her eyes and her ears open for valuable information to aid the Union. Van Lew was adept at secrecy and deception, which allowed her to operate quite effectively even though the townspeople suspected that she was helping the enemy.

Van Lew was an expert in hiding communications so that others would not find them. She hid messages in egg shells, concealed in containers of produce. She wrote other messages in cipher or in invisible ink and transported them in the soles of servants' shoes. The clever Van Lew sent messages in books with words or page numbers lightly underlined. Only one of her messages was ever found.

The eccentric Van Lew also knew how to hide people so that others would not find them. In her Richmond mansion were two hiding places used to house escaped inmates from nearby Libby prison. Although Van Lew's house was searched many times during the Civil War, these hiding places were never discovered until after the war.

Late in the war, Van Lew organized the theft of the body of the Union raider Col. Dahlgren, who was killed in an attempt to free the Libby prison inmates. The Confederates thwarted the scheme and buried Dahlgren secretly, but Van Lew discovered the burial site, had the body exhumed and reburied in a place she thought would be safer. She kept the location of the body a secret until after the war, when the boy's remains were returned to his family.

So skillful was Van Lew at keeping things hidden, that at one time she even managed to hide her horse. When, in the final months of the war, the Confederates were ransacking the South to replace horses for its soldiers, Van Lew rolled up her Oriental carpets and led her horse into the parlor of her home. There the horse stayed hidden while the Confederates searched only the stables (Larson 21-27, Roberts 126).

MORGAN'S TRICKERY

On his famous raid through Indiana in July, 1863, John Morgan with 350 of his guerrillas dashed into a small town, where the raiders came upon about 300 mounted home guards awaiting orders from their aged captain.

"Whose company is this?" demanded the old captain of Morgan.

"This is Wolford's cavalry of Kentucky," lied Morgan. "What are you going to do with all these men and horses?"

"You see, that horse-thieving John Morgan and his band of cut-throats and thieves is in this part of the country, and if he comes this way, we're wantin' to be ready for 'em," the captain replied.

"Morgan's hard to catch. We've been after him for fourteen days and haven't seen him at all," said Morgan.

"If our horses stand fire, we'll be ready for 'em," said the old captain.

"Won't they stand?"

"No, Cap'n Wolford, but I'm told you're a hoss on the drill. While you rest your hosses, why don't you saddle up ours 'n give 'em a lesson."

The Raiders went to work, tying up their weary, worn-out horses to the fence, and saddling up the fresh mounts. The home guard were delighted to think that their pet horses would be trained by Wolford and his men.

"Now, captain, I am ready," said Morgan. "If you and your men wish to witness the training, form a line on each side of the road and watch us closely as we pass," said Morgan.

The captain and his men, as well as some of the ladies from the town, did as they were directed.

"Are you ready?" shouted Morgan to the crowd.

"Ready, Wolford," replied the captain.

"Forward!" shouted Morgan, and the whole column of Morgan's raiders raced through the crowd, some leading a horse or two as they went, leaving their spent horses tied to the fence rails. They never returned.

The company of home guard disbanded that night, but the captain held the horses as prisoners of war. Not a man in the town would ever own up to being tricked out of his horse by John Morgan and his gang (Botkin 289-91).

THE SPOTTED COW

S oldiers were often compelled to resort to extreme measures in order to obtain food for themselves and their horses during a campaign. In times of short rations, foraging became a necessary means for survival for both armies. Common forms of foraging included raiding the sutler's cart, soliciting dinner invitations in nearby homes, and "charging" goods from a country store (McCutcheon 235). But by far the most widespread foraging activity was stealing vegetables and livestock from nearby farms. When foraging parties were sent out to the surrounding countryside, they often made a ludicrous appearance on return to camp, with hay or bags of corn slung over saddles, bound chickens and geese struggling to get loose, and balky livestock in tow. For the most part, foraging was considered a "fun" activity for the soldiers, and those who were detailed to foraging parties were envied by the others who were kept at more mundane camp duties (Forbes 70). However, foraging parties were the bane of the farmers, most of whom never received payment for the stolen property.

After the destructive raid on Holly Springs, Mississippi, in December of 1862, in which all of Grant's army's stores were destroyed, the Union troops found themselves without rations. A young soldier named Hans was assigned to the foraging party, and riding out, he soon spied a handsome spotted cow which he and his comrades captured, slaughtered, skinned, dressed, and took to camp to be cooked and eaten. Hans claimed the spotted hide as his own, since it was, after all, he who had first spotted the cow, and he took it to a tannery in a town nearby.

"How much do you pay for a hide?" Hans asked the tanner.

"Three dollars for a good one," replied the tanner. Hans threw down the spotted hide for the tanner's inspection, and suddenly the man broke into a rage.

"You Yankee thief! You have killed my spotted cow, the last of my cows, and now you ask me to buy the hide!"

The man grabbed at the hide, but Hans persisted.

"Maybe the cow was yours, but now the hide is mine, and you must pay me three dollars if you want it," said Hans.

The tanner being a wise man, thought about the division of Yankees camped practically on his property, and decided it would be useless to argue with the young Yankee soldier. So he paid Hans three dollars for the hide of his last cow, a spotted cow that just a few hours before grazed peacefully in his pasture (Botkin 115-116).

Cavalry Foragers, sketched by Edwin Forbes.

GHOSTS AT BULL RUN

U nion Private Isaac W. Scherich was relieved that it was someone else's turn for picket duty on the old Bull Run Battlefield in October of 1863. The battlefield was said to be haunted by the ghosts of the men killed there in July 1861. After that battle, the dead were not buried for several days after the fighting ceased, and all the interment that many got was loose dirt thrown over their bodies where they had fallen. Over time the rains had washed the dirt away, leaving bare skeletons upon the field. It was enough to make any man shiver.

Private Scherich watched as two of his comrades rode off down the Sudley Springs Road for picket duty, and then he went to bed. Scherich slept through the thunderstorm and heavy rain during the night, but just before dawn he was awakened by the sound of shots coming from the picket post. Soon the two pickets came in at full speed, saying that something white had appeared in front of them. The Sergeant cussed the men out for being cowards, and then ordered Scherich to take picket duty for the rest of the night. Scherich remembered his own ghostly encounter:

> It still continued to rain... I was not there long until a sharp flash of lightening revealed of what the ghost consisted. A flock of six or eight sheep huddled together, which on the noise of the thunder scared and they would run a short dis-

tance and then stop when the noise stopped. Just
as daylight was appearing my relief came and I
told them about the ghosts, which had gone over
the hill by that time. The Sergeant was very
anxious to see them for himself, they were found
and the whole post had mutton for breakfast. The
two scared boys enjoyed the eat just as much as
the others, but it was a long time before they
heard the last of their ghosts.

BIRD'S-EYE VIEW

When the 8th Wisconsin marched into battle, their mascot eagle Old Abe went with them, carried on a perch right beside the regimental colors. The specially built perch was a shield in the shape of a heart on which was inscribed "stars and stripes." A few inches above the shield was a cross piece for the roost, and on each end of it were three arrows pointing outward, representing war as in the great seal of the U.S.(Barrett 26).

When the shooting started, Old Abe soared high above the battlefield, but most of the time in camp he stayed on his perch. Old Abe's battle instincts were acute. At the battle of Farmington in May of 1862, the men were ordered to lie down to take cover. Old Abe insisted on being protected as well, and left his perch and flattened himself on the ground and remained there until the men arose (Barrett 34). He feared artillery fire for a good reason--three of his bearers were shot from under him, and Old Abe himself was wounded at the battle of Vicksburg.

In camp, the eagle followed his master like a puppy, but he developed an intense dislike for the regimental dog, Frank. One day when Frank came within the reach of Abe's tether cord, the bird attacked him. After that, Frank kept a respectful distance (Barrett 31-32).

Old Abe reportedly had a fondness for strong drink. One day a soldier left a cup of peach brandy on the ground for a few moments while the soldier attended to some camp duty. Abe "took a glass, and, in a little while, was intoxicated after the usual style of hard drinkers. He lolled his head and tried to vomit, flapped his wings heavily upon the ground, rolled over, and behaved in an unbecoming manner for an Eagle!" (qtd. in Barrett 70).

But it was after the war that Old Abe became the most celebrated. When his regiment was mustered out in 1864, Old Abe was sent to the state capital in Madison, where he enjoyed a pleasant and well lighted suite in the basement of the Capitol. Here, he enjoyed the company of a beautiful red rooster which had been given to him for his dinner one evening, but which he decided to spare. The rooster and Abe became fast friends, playing and roosting together on the same perch (Barrett 93). Old Abe lived at the Capitol for many years, entertaining important visitors of state and inspiring poets to pen verse about his wartime exploits.

Twenty years after having gone off to war, the very old Abe was trapped when the Capitol burned. Overcome by smoke, Abe was put into the arms of his keeper to die on February 27, 1904 (another source says he died in 1881). Old Abe's remains were sent to the taxidermist, and he is now on display at the Wisconsin State Museum where millions regard him as the ultimate symbol of American courage and strength. In the world famous Atlanta Cyclorama centerpiece painting, Old Abe can be seen flying over the hotly contested battlefield (Robertson, Tenting 151; Davis 136; Garrison, Curiosities 86).

"OLD ABE."

WAR LYRICS

'Tis many a stormy day
Since, out of the cold, bleak North,
Our great War-Eagle sailed forth
To swoop o'er battle and fray.
Many and many a day
O'er charge and storm hath he wheeled,
Foray and foughten field,
Tramp, and volley and rattle!--
Over crimson trench and turf,
Over climbing clouds of surf,
Through tempest and cannon-rack,
Have his terrible pinions whirled--
(A thousand fields of battle!
A million leagues of foam!)
But our Bird shall yet come back,
He shall soar to his Eyrie-Home--
And his thunderous wing be furled,
In the gaze of a gladdened world,
On the Nation's loftiest Dome!"

--Henry Howard Brownell

STINGING ENCOUNTER

Union Brigadier General William French was known to his men as *old blink-eye* because of his habit of batting his eyes when he talked. During the battle of Antietam, French and his men encountered a line of Confederate skirmishers on the farm of William Roulette and his family. One of French's ten regiments was the 132nd Pennsylvania, a "green" regiment that was facing combat for the first time. French watched his men advance against the enemy, when suddenly the men of the 132nd Pennsylvania broke formation and began to swat themselves furiously. Around the men swarmed hundreds of thousands of angry honey bees that were irritated when a shell destroyed their hives in the Roulette apiary. But the men of the 132nd Pennsylvania went on to face a more formidable enemy later that same day. In less than an hour of fighting, nearly one third of French's division fell while trying to penetrate Confederate defenses in the sunken road that would forever after be called Bloody Lane (Bailey 93).

A Land Flowing with Milk and Honey, sketched by
Edwin Forbes. (Dover Pictorial Archives)

THE COCKY REBEL

J ake Donelson, Company H, 3rd Tennessee Regiment, was one cocky Rebel, even as a prisoner of war. Jake, a young red rooster, escaped the stewpot when he was purchased by Sgt. Jerome B. McCanless early in the war. McCanless was so taken by the bird that he made Jake his personal mascot. Jake did not escape prison, however, when the Confederate army surrendered to Grant at Fort Donelson on Feb. 16, 1862. Jake and his master were then taken to Vicksburg and exchanged.

Back in camp, McCanless hired an artist to paint a portrait of his feathered friend Jake, and after the war McCanless reportedly carried the 13x16-inch image to many reunions of Confederate veterans. That portrait now hangs in the home of Attorney General McCanless of Nashville, and Jake's military history is inscribed in a brass plate beneath the portrait.

As for Jake, he died in 1864 and was given a military burial with honors. McCanless served until the end of the war, taking part in the Vicksburg, Atlanta and Nashville Campaigns, and died in 1906 (Nye 28).

HORSE
OF A DIFFERENT COLOR

When the first call for Union enlistments went out, S. Emma Edmonds wanted to answer, so she cut off her hair, got into a man's suit, took the name of Frank Thompson, and tried to enlist. After four tries, Emma was finally sworn in, and she became one of about 400 women who succeeded in enlisting on both sides during the great confrontation.

Emma, alias Private Frank Thompson, served as a male nurse in the 2nd Volunteers (Michigan) of the United States Army, and according to her memoirs, her true gender was never discovered during the course of the war. When McClellan's staff put out the word that they were looking for a person to serve as a spy, Emma volunteered. She studied all she could find out about military operations and at her interview she so impressed the staff that they gave her the job.

Emma, alias Frank, successfully infiltrated the Confederate lines several times during her stint as a spy under the cover of some ingenious disguises. On one mission, Emma disguised herself as an Irish peddler woman. Under the ruse of selling her wares, Emma gathered as much information as she could and returned to the Union camp on a stolen Confederate horse she called Rebel (Markle 175-77).

In her memoirs published after the war (Emma resumed her female identity upon leaving the army),

Emma recounted her adventures and told of the special bond she felt for her war horses. She credited one of these loyal animals with saving her life:

> I traveled till two o'clock in the morning, when my horse began to show signs of giving out; then I stopped at a farm house, but not being able to make any one hear me, I hitched my horse under cover of a wood-shed, and taking the blanket from under the saddle, I lay down beside him, the saddle-blanket being my only covering. The storm had ceased, but the night was intensely cold, and the snow was about two or three inches deep. I shall always believe that I would have perished that night, had not my faithful horse lain down beside me, and by the heat of his beautiful head, which he laid across my shoulders, (a thing which he always did whenever I lay down where he could reach me) kept me from perishing in my wet clothes." (Edmonds 293)

Ironically, the next day, Emma's loyal horse was shot from under her by a Confederate guerilla. The horse died with his head upon Emma's shoulders and the Confederates left Emma for dead (Edmonds 295).

Emma Underneath her Dead Horse. (From her war memoirs, *The Female Spy of the Union Army*.)

CLAIRVOYANT KITTY

Louis Newcome was only fourteen when he joined a Union regiment as a drummer boy and headed for the front. Not long after, according to memoirs penned after the war, Newcome became a Union spy at President Lincoln's request, and in the company of his mare, Kitty, and dog, Tige, set out on a series of dangerous missions delivering cipher dispatches across enemy lines. Newcome was especially attached to Kitty and gives her credit for saving his life on several occasions. About one of these incidents, Newcome wrote:

> As we went on I began to feel very sleepy. I could hardly keep my eyes open. At last I simply had to dismount. I found a sheltered spot and, taking the blanket off the mare, rolled in it and fell into a heavy sleep. Kitty kept watch over me. Maybe you don't believe it, but nevertheless it is true. I suppose I had been sleeping about two or more hours when I was awakened by the mare nosing me in the neck. I was on my feet in a moment. Some men were talking. I crawled over to the road and saw five men passing. I couldn't be sure but I think they were Mosby's men. (Newcome 84-85)

When Newcome was fully awake, he resumed his journey through Spotsyvania County. Suddenly, Kitty stopped and refused to go further. The mare shied into the woods, not heeding the boy's command to continue. Newcome writes: "I tried to stop her but she went on. 'You know better than I do,' I said, and let her have her head--just in time to avoid a large body of cavalry. As they passed I grabbed Kitty by the nose to stop her from neighing in answer to some horse in the troop, but not a whimper came from her. From the time we started on this trip, Kitty seemed to know something was up." (Newcome 84-85)

MULE HEROES

In her wartime memoirs, S. Emma Edmonds notes
how she enjoyed watching the long trains of six-
mules teams which were constantly passing and
repassing within a few yards of her tent. With character-
istic humor, Emma notes that mules, like people, could
be sorted into several "classes" depending on their
personality traits. Emma was reminded of a Miss Peri-
winkle's remarks about the classes of mules:

> The coquettish mule has small feet, a nicely
> trimmed tail, perked up ears, and seems much
> given to little tosses of the head, affected skips and
> prances, and if he wears bells or streamers, puts
> on as many airs as any belle. The moral mule is a
> stout, hardworking creature, always tugging with
> all his might, often pulling away after the rest
> have stopped, laboring under the conscientious
> delusion that food for the entire army depends
> upon his individual exertions. The histrionic mule
> is a melo-dramatic (sic) sort of quadruped, prone
> to startle humanity by erratic leaps and wild
> plunges, much shaking of the stubborn head and
> lashing of his vicious heels; now and then falling
> flat, and apparently dying a la Forrest, a gasp, a
> groan, a shudder, etc. till the street is blocked up,
> the drivers all swearing like so many demons, and
> the chief actor's circulation becomes   decidedly

quickened by every variety of kick, cuff and jerk imaginable. When the last breath seems to have gone with the last kick, and the harness has been taken off, then a sudden resurrection takes place. He springs to his feet, and proceeds to give himself two or three comfortable shakes, and if ever a mule laughed in scornful triumph it is he, and as he calmly surveys the excited crowd, seems to say: 'A hit! a decided hit!' For once the most stupid of all animals has outwitted more than a dozen lords of creation.

The pathetic mule is, perhaps, the most interesting of all; for although he always seems to be the smallest, thinnest, and weakest of the six, yet, in addition to his equal portion of the heavy load, he carries on his back a great postilion, with tremendous boots, long tailed coat, and heavy whip. This poor creature struggles feebly along, head down, coat muddy and rough, eye spiritless and sad, and his whole appearance a perfect picture of meek misery, fit to touch a heart of stone. Then there is another class of mules which always have a jolly, cheer-up sort of look about them--they take everything good naturedly, from cudgeling tocaressing, and march along with a roguish twinkle in their eye which is very interesting. (qtd. in Edmonds 75-77)

Confederate Private Sam Watkins' memoirs also detail a number of mule anecdotes, including an incident that took place at Shiloh: "One fellow, a courier, who had had his horse killed, got on a mule he had captured, and in the last charge, before the final and fatal halt was made, just charged right ahead by his lone self, and the soldiers said, 'Just look at that brave man, charging right in the jaws of death.' He began to seesaw the mule and grit his teeth, and finally yelled out, 'It arn't me, boys, it's this blarsted old mule. Whoa! Whoa!'" (Watkins 67)

Despite the temperamental nature of mules, both armies depended on the hardy animals to pull heavy loads, often in adverse weather conditions. There is no doubt that many of these animals suffered at the hands of their human masters. A pair of Texas mules, for example, became the victims of a particularly cruel scheme to "mow down boys in gray like ripe wheat." Captain James Graydon ordered his men to pack a number of 24-pound howitzer shells into wood boxes and then lash them to the backs of a pair of mules. Under cover of darkness, Graydon's men moved across a river with the animals. When they were within 150 yards of the unsuspecting Confederates, the Federals lit the fuses, gave each animal a hard smack on the rear, and ran for their own lines. The mules moved into action-- they turned and followed their drivers instead of going forward towards the Confederates. One observer wrote: "Every one of them shells exploded on time, but there were only two casualties--the mules" (Garrison, Curiosities 144-5).

In another instance, a pack of mules helped to win a battle. When Longstreet and his troops reached Wauhat-chie in the middle of a cool October night, they made an almost immediate attack on Geary's division of Hooker's forces. During the three-hour fight, Geary's mules became panic stricken by the sounds of battle raging around them. In the mayhem, the frightened mules broke loose and stampeded towards the enemy, rushing pell mell across the field towards Longstreet's startled men. Believing that it was a cavalry charge, Longstreet's line broke and fled. After the battle, the quartermaster in charge of the stampeding mules sent the following message to headquarters: "I respectfully request that the mules, for their gallantry in this action, may have conferred upon them the brevet rank of horses." General Grant reportedly laughed heartily at the suggestion (Botkin 333).

Mule Team Crossing a Stream (Frank Leslie's Illustrated)

SEE SPOT RUN

Like all Civil War prison camps, Andersonville was a miserable place. Time passed slowly for the men who were kept there. Flies, mosquitoes and lice pestered the prisoners. Food and water and personal space were scarce. At times the temperatures exceeded 100 degrees, and the sweltering humidity of the Georgia climate was unbearable. The deplorable conditions sometimes caused the men to go insane or even to seek death as an escape.

At Andersonville, Captain Henry Wirz, the officer in charge, ordered the construction of a "deadline." This row of three-foot wooden posts set up 19 feet inside the stockade wall was intended to prevent escapes. Guards were ordered to shoot any prisoner who crossed the deadline. Prisoner John Ranson wrote, "Men are continuously going up to the dead line and getting shot. They do not get much sympathy, as they should know better" (qtd. in Burnett 9).

Escape was often on the minds of the desperate prisoners. Several attempted to tunnel out of prison in July of 1864. According to Samuel Burdick, Private, Co. H, 17th Iowa Infantry, "Today a tunnel was discovered by the rebel authorities. Four of the prisoners had dug a well 60 feet deep about 20 feet down they had struck out dug 20 feet out side the stockade and were a going to escape in 10 nights, one of our men betrayed them for a plug of tobacco" (qtd. in Burnett 27).

Those prisoners who managed to escape from Andersonville could expect to be tracked by bloodhounds once trained to retrieve escaping slaves. According to Josiah Brownell, Private, "A man named Turner, who lived near the prison kept a pack of bloodhounds, and he was employed by Capt. Wirz to catch those who escaped. Every morning at daylight the dogs were called together, and with their master, who was mounted on a large bay horse, they made a circuit of the prison" (qtd. in Burnett 18).

One of the most fearful of these dogs was known as "Spot." The reverse of Spot's carte d'visite made after the war tells the horrible tale of the fate of those escapees who encountered the animal: "Weight, 159 pounds: height, 3 feet; length from tip to tip, 6 feet 4 1/2 inches. This dog is a Cuban Bloodhound; and was one of a pack of thirteen hounds (some of them, however, being ordinary Southern hounds) used by Captain Wirtz (sic), at Andersonville Prison, Ga., for the purpose of recapturing Union prisoners who had escaped, and who were frequently killed or badly mutilated by these dogs. Eleven of this pack were killed by Union soldiers who went to Andersonville at about the time the war closed; the remaining two were brought North, and one of them has since died, leaving this dog the only survivor. Photographed by J. W. Turner, No. 47 Hanover Street, Boston."

The association of the guard dogs and Andersonville Prison was so strong, that survivors incorporated the image into their commemorative medals manufactured after the war. The medals show a ferocious guard dog attacking a fleeing prisoner. The inscription reads: Death Before Dishonor.

Spot

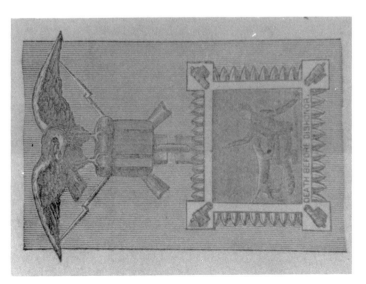

Spot: Line Drawing of a Commemorative medal made after the war, showing guard dog attacking a prisoner. (Both from the collection of Marcus S. McLemore). Sketch of a guard dog attacking an escaped prisoner. (From Boggs, Eighteen Months a Prisoner Under the Rebel Flag.)

HERO
THE HELL HOUND

Andersonville wasn't alone in using dogs to guard prisoners. According to a diary kept by Lt. A. O. Abbott of the First New York Dragoons, Yankee prisoners held at Columbia, South Carolina, axed to death two guard dogs and then hid their bodies in an abandoned well. Soon, the Confederate guards began a search for the dogs and "brought to light the missing dogs--dead bloodhounds that were two of a pack put around camp every morning to discover if any Yankees had made fresh tracks for liberty during the night" (qtd. in Garrison, Curiosities 81).

At Libby Prison and Castle Thunder in Richmond, prisoners were guarded by Hero. At Libby, security was so tight that prisoners feared to look out the windows in case they became the target of the Confederate guards. However, some did escape. In February of 1864, 109 men escaped from Libby Prison by crawling through a hand dug tunnel. Of that total, 48 were recaptured but 61 made their way to freedom.

The reverse side of Hero's carte d'visite gives the animal's history: "Weight, 198 pounds; height, 3 feet 2 inches; length from tip to tip, 7 feet 1 1/2 inches. This dog is a Russian bloodhound; and was imported from Russia in 1859, by a Southern gentleman, for sports of the arena. Soon after the breaking out of the rebellion he was seized by the Rebel government, and subsequently used for guarding Union prisoners, at Libby Prison and Castle Thunder, Richmond, Va. His proportions are enormous, --he is believed to be the largest dog in the world, --and is possessed of prodigious strength. He has been engaged in several bear fights, and was successful in all of them. Photographed by J. W. Turner, No. 47 Hanover Street, Boston."

"Hero."

Hero, Castle Thunder, Libby Prison (Photos from the collection of Marcus S. McLemore)

Part IV:

Ghastly Deaths
and Beastly Burials

Nor dread nor hope attend
A dying animal;
A man awaits his end
Dreading and hoping all.
    --William Butler Yeats

GHASTLY DEATHS
AND BEASTLY BURIALS

Introduction

The aftermath of battle was almost as trying as the fighting itself, as the bone-weary survivors on either side reclaimed their wounded for medical attention and their dead for burial. Burial detail was gruesome. Sometimes, bodies were left uncovered for days, decaying in the heat, or they were only partially buried, and then later exhumed to be reinterred in the deceased's family plot. It might be years before a loved one's body was finally recovered, as at Gettysburg, where removal of the Confederate dead from the original field burial plots was not undertaken until seven years after the battle.

But what of the animals that perished during the war? Sometimes the carcasses were buried or burned, but often they were left to rot. After Antietam, Federal Brigadier General Oliver O. Howard complained about the stench that arose from the swollen bodies of the dead horses. He said, "We tried piling rails and loose limbs of trees upon them and setting the heap on fire. This made the stench only increase in volume" (Bailey 150).

Many soldiers grieved over the loss of their horses as much as they did the loss of their comrades in arms. Confederate General I. R. Trimble, for example, wrote of his loss at Gettysburg: "I was shot through the left leg on horseback near the close of the fight and my fine mare after taking me off the field died of the same shot-- Poor Jinny, noble horse, I grieve to part thus with you" (qtd. in Svenson 208).

Burning Dead Horses After a Battle, sketch by H. Lovie. (Frank Leslie's Illustrated)

HORSE REVISITED

Gradually, the line of fire was extended until the small group of Union soldiers at Newbern was surrounded. Rev. Henry White, Chaplain to the 5th Rhode Island Infantry dismounted and led his horse to a depression in the landscape that might offer the beast some protection from the flying bullets. Solid shot and then canister was being thrown all around them, and White knew that it would only be a matter of minutes before the men of the Rhode Island must surrender and be taken as Confederate prisoners. At half past two, the firing ceased and sixteen hundred Confederates arose from their hiding places as the white flag of surrender was raised from the fort. Rev. White walked among the men of the 5th Rhode Island, comforting the wounded and doing what he could to cheer them in their hopeless despair. When he returned to his horse, Rev. White was heartsick to find that the animal had been mortally wounded. He described the scene in a letter: "...I went down in the rifle pit just outside the fort to take a last look at my noble horse, and found that, although severely wounded, he was not dead. I requested a rebel soldier to put a ball through his head and close his suffering. 'Twas better he should be good for the vultures than bear a rebel, a traitor, an enemy in the seat where a patriot rode" (Jervey 12).

Rev. White was held prisoner at Andersonville and Macon for five months before he was released in September of 1864. One of the first things White did as a free man was return to the Newbern battlefield, where he paid tribute to the remains of his horse. White wrote: "The bones of my horse lay where he fell. The hole in the skull showed where the ball went in that took his life" (Jervey 83-84).

DEAD ON HIS FEET

During a battle, many horses were killed or wounded and later had to be destroyed. Quite often, horses were deliberately shot at by the enemy. After the battle at Antietam (Sharpsburg) in the fall of 1862, Col. Robert Shaw of the 2nd Massachusetts wrote to his wife, Annie: "The number of dead horses scattered about, for a distance of four miles, is enormous. One battery which was placed near us in line that day had sixteen horses killed" (qtd. in Duncan 264). In July of 1863, more than 3,000 horses were killed in the fighting at Gettysburg. One artillery battalion, the 9th Massachusetts, lost 80 of its 88 animals in the Trostle farmyard (Davis 218).

Some Civil War battles were little more than free-for-all slaughters of men and beasts. One witness to the aftermath of battle wrote, "There being no room in the rear, their caissons and limbers stood off to their right on a flat piece of heavily wooded ground. This was almost covered with dead horses. I think there must have been eighty or ninety on less than an acre; one I noticed standing almost upright, perfectly lifeless, supported by a fallen tree" (qtd. in McCutcheon 230).

Confederate private Sam Watkins also remembered a scene of death from the battle of Franklin, Tennessee late in the war:

...we looked over the battlefield, O, my God! what did we see! It was a grand holocaust of death. Death had held high carnival there that night. The dead were piled the one on the other all over the ground. I never was so horrified and appalled in my life. Horses, like men, had died game on the gory breastworks. General Adams' horse had his fore feet on one side of the works and his hind feet on the other, dead. The general seems to have been caught so that he was held to the horse's back, sitting almost as if living, riddled, and mangled with balls (Watkins 219-20).

Sharpshooter Improvising a Rest for his Rifle. (Frank Leslie's Illustrated)

LUCK OF THE DRAW

Confederates usually brought along their own horses when they went off to war, as did the four young Guillet brothers. When one of the brothers was fatally shot as he rode the family horse in battle, the next brother inherited the animal. One by one, the three remaining Guillet brothers were fatally shot as they rode the horse. Young Captain S. Isadore Guillet was the last brother to be killed, but before he died he willed the horse to his nephew, whose fate is unknown (Davis 139).

On the flip side of the coin, some riders were more charmed than their animals. Major General Nathan B. Forrest had three horses shot out from under him within five hours during a battle at Fort Pillow in April of 1864. That's just one less dead horse than the four-year total of Rutherford B. Hayes (Garrison, Treasury 180). Forrest set an all time record for the number of mounts killed under him for the duration of the war. According to his fellow officer, Brig. Gen. James R. Chalmers, no fewer than twenty seven horses were shot under Forrest (Garrison, Curiosities 75).

Maj. Gen. George A. Custer was wounded only once during the Civil War, but eleven horses were shot from under him. One of his fellow officers, Brig. Gen. Charles R. Lowell, lost an even dozen mounts. Confederate Maj. Gen. Joseph Wheeler had sixteen horses killed under him (Garrison, Curiosities 75).

Many officers refused to ride a white horse because it made a tempting target for the enemy sharpshooters. Exceptions included confederate Brig. Gen. Thomas F. Drayton who rode his favorite white war horse at Hilton Head, South Carolina. "Fighting Joe" Hooker rode a white horse at Antietam, claiming that the horse made it easy for his men to identify him. At Fort Donelson, Capt. T. L. Newsham rode along the Union front, mounted on a white horse. Later, Union Lt. Jim Coughlan led charges at Resaca mounted on a white horse (Garrison, Curiosities 73-74).

Rebel Mules Killed by Federal shell. (Library of Congress)

REQUIEM FOR A ROOSTER

T he men of Company H, First Tennessee Regiment, were awakened every morning by the crowing of a rooster named "Fed" for Confederacy. Fed belonged to Tom Tuck, who carried the cock in his haversack. More than just the company mascot, Fed was a trained fighter with a reputation for winning in the cruel sport of cock fighting. During cock fights, each bird is fitted with gaffs, or long pieces of razor sharp steel placed over the rooster's spurs. Then the two roosters are placed into the gaming pit and held close enough together until they are sufficiently angry to fight. It was in a match such as this that poor Fed finally met his match when his opponent slashed both gaffs into Fed's head.

When Private Tuck saw that his prized rooster was dead, he picked up the animal and said:

> Poor Fed, I loved you; you used to crow every morning at daylight to wake me up. I have carried you a long time, but, alas! alas! poor Fed, your days are numbered, and those who fight will sometimes be slain. Now, friends, conscripts, countrymen, if you have any tears to shed, prepare to shed them now. I will not bury Fed. The evil that roosters do live after them, but the good is oft interred with their bones. So let it not be with Confed. Confed left no will, but I will pick him, fry him, and dip my biscuit in his gravy. Poor Fed,

Confed, Confederacy, I place one hand on my heart and one on my head, regretting that I have not another to place on my stomach and whisper, softly whisper , in the most doleful accents, Good-bye, farewell, a long farewell. (qtd. in Watkins 188-89)

In his memoirs, Private Sam Watkins versifies Fed's funeral ceremony (189):

Not a laugh was heard--not even a joke--
As the dead rooster in the camp-kettle they hurried;
For Tom had lost ten dollars, and was broke,
In the cock-pit where Confed was buried.

They cooked him slowly in the middle of the day,
As the frying-pan they were solemnly turning;
The hungry fellows looking at him as he lay,
With one side raw, the other burning.

Some surplus feathers covered his breast,
Not in a shroud, but in a tiara they soused him;
He lay like a 'picked chicken' taking his rest,
While the Rebel boys danced and cursed around him.

Not a few or short were the cuss words they said,
Yet, they spoke many words of sorrow;
As they steadfastly gazed on the face of the dead,
And thought 'what'll we do for chicken tomorrow?'

Lightly they'll talk of the Southern confed that's gone,
And o'er his empty carcass upbraid him;
But nothing he'll reck, if they let him sleep on,
In the place where they have laid him.

Sadly and slowly they laid him down,
From the field of the fame fresh and gory;
They ate off his flesh, and threw away his bones,
And then left them alone in their glory.

Apparently, the mourners were interrupted by a Yankee raid in the middle of the funeral feast, for Sam Watkins writes that in the end, poor Fed sank so low as to become food for the Federals.

SEA HORSE

The crowd lining the parade route in Boston on May 28, 1864, watched and waited beneath the cloudless sky. Finally they saw what they had been waiting for, as down the street marched a thousand dark-skinned soldiers in arms, the 54th Massachusetts, the nation's first all-black fighting regiment. The crowd cheered as the soldiers approached, led by mounted riders, two bands and a drum corps. The white officers included the commander, the youthful Col. Robert Gould Shaw and his officer Major Edward Needles Hallowell. Each man was mounted on his favorite horse, and observer John Greenleaf Whittier remembered thinking that Shaw seemed as "beautiful and awful as an angel of God come down to lead the host of freedom to victory" (qtd. in Duncan 40).

Later that day, the 54th Massachusetts had orders to board the transport steamer DeMolay, which would carry the regiment and their mounts to Hilton Head, South Carolina. The trip would take one week. On the fifth day out, the DeMolay steamed past Charleston where the passengers saw the blockading fleet and Fort Sumter. Later that day, they were struck with a violent thunderstorm, and the men were amazed at its fury. Many men were treated for seasickness but despite the violent storm, there was only one fatality the entire trip, On June 1, 1863, Col. Shaw described the event in a letter to his wife, Annie:

Off Cape Hatteras... We have got thus far
on our voyage without accident, excepting
the loss of Major Hallowell's mare, which
died this morning, and was consigned to
the sea. (qtd. in Duncan 334)

Shaw later wrote that he planned to sell Hallowell,
one of the three horses he had brought along with him.
Shaw was killed a few weeks later when the 54th
assaulted Fort Wagner, but Hallowell was among the
survivors of that battle.

Boston's Robert Gould Shaw/54th Regiment Memorial (Greater
Boston Convention & Visitors Bureau, Inc.)

SHOOT TO KILL

Perhaps no other figure of the Civil War is associated with more destruction and brutality than the Union's Major General William Tecumseh Sherman. The scruffy looking warrior rode a horse named Sam. After the burning of Atlanta in September of 1864, Sherman began his famous march to the sea. His apparent aim was destruction.

In parts of Georgia, Sherman was hailed by the slaves as the deliverer promised in the Bible. Some considered Sherman and his men as avenging angels. At one plantation owned by the Farrar family, slaves told Major Henry Hitchcock that they had been habitually flogged with straps, handsaws and paddles, and salt put into their wounds. The Farrar slaves also spoke of a large red bloodhound at the next plantation, used to hunt runaway slaves. Sherman ordered his men to shoot the hell hound.

Sherman's men killed tracking dogs whenever they found them as they continued their march to the sea because they believed the dogs had been used to track escaping Federal prisoners as well as runaway slaves. The soldiers frequently killed domestic pets as well, but they kept some of these critters--dogs, cats, gamecocks, goats, donkeys, raccoons, possums, and pigs--as pets of their own (Nevin 59-60).

Most of the civilian animals killed by soldiers, however, were slaughtered as food for the hungry army passing through. Some Yankee soldiers claimed that the meat they were being issued in camp was not beef at all, but mule. One Connecticut soldier stated that "the commissary at Annapolis has given us so much mule meat that the ears of the whole regiment have grown three and a half inches since their arrival at the Maryland capital" (qtd. in Wiley, Yank 240).

A group of Yankees who received a particularly bad lot of meat decided to "lay it to rest" with honor due to long service in the army. Laying the rotten meat inside a hardtack box, they surrounded it with scraps of harness for proper identity, and marched with it in martial procession to its final resting place in the camp dump where soldiers fired the customary fusillade over the grave (Wiley, Yank 240).

So it was no wonder that soldiers often foraged for better fare from civilians in the surrounding countryside. An Ohio soldier wrote that he could not help chasing Southern chickens, and added "they are always sure to cackle at the Stars and Stripes and that would not do" (qtd. in Wiley, Yank 236).

Another story told of a forager coming into camp with a hen and a goose hanging from his rifle. An officer reproached him for robbing civilians of their animals, but the forager replied: "Oh! bedad Srr, this goose came out as I was wending my way along placable and hissed at the American flag, and bejabez I shot him on the spot... and I found this hen laying eggs for the Ribil (sic) Army, and I hit her a whack that stopped that act of treason on the spot, too" (qtd. in Wiley, Yank 236).

This magic lantern slide depicts in color a scene showing a blood-hound that has tracked down a runaway slave. The Union officer stands in defiance of the plantation owner who wants to reclaim his property. (From the collection of Marcus S. McLemore)

RECIPE FOR RAT

I n the field, Yankee messes consisted of four to eight men, each of whom took his turn as "dogrobber" or cook. Hunger and shortage of fresh meat often caused the dogrobbers to experiment with the culinary. Hungry Yanks in Louisiana, for example, converted the tail of an alligator into a soup that they said was very good. Other soldiers reported eating rattlesnakes, and fried jaybirds and red headed woodpeckers (Wiley, Yank 244).

Hungry Confederates in Vicksburg reportedly feasted on rats when rations became scant. Private Sam Watkins described the capture and preparation of this delicacy:

> Presently we came to an old outhouse that seemed to be a natural harbor for this kind of vermin. The house was quickly torn down and out jumped an old residenter, who was old and gray... After chasing him backwards and forwards, the rat finally got tired of this foolishness and started for his hole. But a rat's tail is the last that goes in the hole, and as he went in we made a grab for his tail. Well, tail hold broke, and we held the skin of his tail in our hands. But we were determined to have that rat. After hard work we caught him. We skinned him, washed and salted him, buttered and peppered him, and fried him. He actually looked nice. The delicate aroma of frying rat came to our hungry nostrils. We were keen to eat a piece of

rat; our teeth were on edge; yea, even our mouths watered to eat a piece of rat. Well, after a while he was said to be done. I got a piece of cold corn dodger, laid my piece of the rat on it, eat a little piece of the bread, and raised the piece of rat to my mouth, when I happened to think of how that rat's tail did slip. I had lost my appetite for dead rat. I did not eat any rat. It was my first and last effort to eat dead rats. (Watkins 108-9)

MARINE DISASTER

Everybody aboard! Everybody aboard!" shouted the Federal officer in charge of transportation at Vicksburg. Nearly 2,000 happy Civil War veterans swarmed aboard the paddle-wheel steamer Sultana at Vicksburg, Mississippi, elated that the war was finally over and the killing done. The Sultana also carried nearly 100 horses and mules, as well as 100 hogs, and one alligator in a wooden crate.

The Sultana was riding low in the water on April 25, 1865, before the last 500 or so crowded aboard for the trip north to the Illinois railhead. From there the Civil War survivors would head home to their loved ones. Little did they know, in the euphoria of that post-war day, that disaster was but a few hours away.

In the predawn hours of April 27, the Sultana steamed her way through the cluster of islands called Paddy's Hens and Chickens. Suddenly, the overheated boiler blasted its way through the boat's side, blowing equipment, men and animals into the sky. The nearest shore was a mile and a half away in either direction, and men clung to floating debris in their fight for survival. A few managed to swim to safety, but more than one veteran owed his life to the animals aboard. Seaman William Lugenbeal snatched up his bayonet, killed the alligator, and drifted to shore holding tightly to the alligator's crate. Some men were saved by clinging to the tails of the mules.

In a little more than an hour after the explosion, the decks of the Sultana were empty of any living man or animal. At sunrise, the smoking skeleton of the steamboat hit an island and sank into the Mississippi. Some of the dead bodies were not recovered until weeks after the disaster.

According to officials in Memphis, 1,547 persons died in the disaster. Combined Union and Confederate deaths at First Bull Run were slightly over half of the Sultana's total. Not even the sinking of the Titanic took so many American lives as the Sultana disaster. Ironically, the incident received little media attention because on the same day, John Wilkes Booth, Lincoln's assassin, had been apprehended and killed (Garrison, Treasury 231-234).

OLD BALDY

I n September of 1861, General Meade purchased a horse from Colonel David Hunter for $150. Meade named the animal Old Baldy because the beast had a white face.

Old Baldy saw action in the battles of First and Second Bull Run, Antietam, Fredericksburg, Mine Run, Chancellorsville, Gettysburg, The Wilderness, Cold Harbor, Bristoe Station, and Petersburg. Reportedly, the horse was wounded no fewer than five, perhaps as many as fourteen times. When Old Baldy was struck in the ribs by a shell in action at Weldon Railroad, General Meade finally decided to retire his faithful mount to a farm near Philadelphia.

When the war ended, Old Baldy enjoyed the glory that came with being a vertan war horse. Old Baldy enjoyed visits from General Meade at the farm, and he participated in many memorial parades. When General Meade died, Old Baldy even participated in the military funeral of his master. But the dignity of the horse's life did not extend to his death.

At the age of thirty, when he was too feeble to stand, Old Baldy was put to sleep and buried. A week later, two of Meade's veterans dug up Old Baldy, cut off his head, and turned it over to a taxidermist. Today, Old Baldy's head is mounted in a special glass case in the Meade Room of the Civil War Library and Museum in

Philadelphia where it is cared for by the Old Baldy Civil War Round Table (Magner 6-7).

TRAVELLER'S BONES

Perhaps the most famous Civil War mount, in monument and in paintings at least, is Lee's horse, Traveller. Lee purchased the horse for $200 in 1861, and Traveller became Lee's favorite war horse throughout the conflict. According to Lee's own account:

> He carried me through the seven days battle around Richmond, the Second Manassas, at Sharpsburg, Fredericksburg, the last day at Chancellorsville, to Penna, at Gettysburg and back to the Rappahannock. From commencement of the campaign in 1864 at Orange, till its close around Petersburg, the saddle was scarcely off his back, as he passed through the fire of the Wilderness, Spotsylvania, Cold Harbour, and across the James River. He was almost in daily requisition in the winter of 1864-65 on the long line of defenses from the Chickahominy north of Richmond, to Hatcher's run south of the Appomattox, 35 miles in length; and in 1865 bore me to the final days at Appomattox Ct. House. (qtd. in Freeman, vol. 1, 645-646)

After the war, Lee had a spacious brick stable built for Traveller next to his house in Lexington. Unfortunately Lee's horse became the target of souvenir hunters who tore away so much of the horse's tail hair that Traveller became nervous and wouldn't allow anyone to stand behind him.

The faithful Traveller outlived Lee and on the day that Lee was buried, the horse walked directly behind the hearse. Several years later, Traveller died of lockjaw, to the great distress of the Lee family who had Traveller's remains buried on the property of Washington and Lee University. In 1907, Traveller's bones were disinterred and his reconstructed skeleton was put on display in the university museum (Freeman, vol. 1, 644-647).

The bones were finally laid to rest in the 1970's, when Traveller was reburied on school grounds.

General Robert E. Lee on Traveller (Library of Congress: LCUSZ62-10805)

Note: This famous photograph of Lee on Traveller was taken in 1866 by Miley. It has become one of the most popular photographs of the Civil War.

After the War, an artist requested a description of Traveller, so Lee dictated this loving description of the war horse that had served him so well:

> If I were an artist like you I would draw a true picture of Traveller--representing his fine proportions, muscular figure, deep chest and short back, strong haunches, flat legs, small head, broad forehead, delicate ears, quick eye, small feet, and black mane and tail. Such a picture would inspire a poet, whose genius could then depict his worth and describe his endurance of toil, hunger, thirst, heat, cold, and the dangers and sufferings through which he passed. He could dilate up on his sagacity and affection, and his invariable response to every wish of his rider. He might even imagine his thoughts, through the long night marches and days of battle through which he has passed. But I am no artist; I can only say he is a Confederate gray. I purchased him in the mountains of Virginia in the autumn of 1861, and he has been my patient follower ever since... You must know the comfort he is to me in my present retirement... You can, I am sure, from what I have said, paint his portrait. (qtd. in Photographic History 120)

GRAVE MATTERS

G en. Stonewall Jackson loved his war horse Little Sorrel, whom he called "Fancy." The horse had so easy a gait that Jackson occasionally slept on the horse when the army was on a march. Little Sorrel was also popular with the Southern ladies and had to be protected from admirers who tried to cut the hair from his mane and tail to make souvenir bracelets.

Unlike his owner, Little Sorrel survived the war. Until recently, the bones of Little Sorrel were stored in a back room of the Virginia Military Institute. Nearly 111 years after Little Sorrel's death, the Virginia Division of the United Daughters of the Confederacy and VMI decided to inter the remains with full honors.

On July 20, 1997, a processional marched from Jackson Memorial (where Little sorrel's brown hide is mounted over plaster of Paris in a permanent display in the basement museum) to the life-size bronze statue of Jackson at the head of the parade ground. Here, the cremated bones of Little Sorrel were laid to rest. The Fincastle Rifles, a re-enactment group, fired three volleys as the remains were lowered into the grave by four men dressed as Confederate soldiers. When the ceremony was ended, some of the 300 or so observers pitched into the grave dirt gathered from Civil War battlefields.

Ironically, the grave of Little Sorrel is located a few hundred yards away from the grave of Robert E. Lee's horse, Traveller. According to one observer, "...in matters grave, Lexington no longer can be called a one-horse town" (Finn).

ACKNOWLEDGMENTS

I t's considered risky business for a non-historian (such as myself) to tackle a topic as complex as the American Civil War. Nevertheless, feeling strongly enough about the contents of this book to seek its publication, I asked historian Dr. Leonne Hudson of Kent State University to read over the manuscript to ascertain that I had not made any major blunders. I am grateful for his advice and encouragement, and have incorporated his wise suggestions into this book. Any errors or omissions are absolutely my own.

Thanks also to Marcus S. McLemore whose war dogs display at a Civil War show in Mansfield, Ohio, sparked my interest in some of the battlefield and prison dogs I had not read about. Marcus, a Civil War researcher and collector, generously granted permission for some of the material in his private collection to be photographed for publication in this book. He is the owner of McLemore's Canine Training and Kennel in Poland, Ohio.

I am grateful to David Dreier, Facility Manager of the Gettysburg National Military Park, for securing the photo of Sallie the dog; and to the Western Reserve Historical Society for granting permission to publish two illustrations from their collection.

Once again, I am indebted to my friend Jane Ann Turzillo, photographer and writer, for her encouragement on this project right from the beginning. Jane accompanied me on many visits to Civil War sites, including Johnson's Island and the battlefields of Gettysburg, Antietam, Bull Run and Fredericksburg. In addition to helping me gather material for this book, Jane read early versions of the manuscript and advised me during revision.

As always, I am grateful for the loving encouragement of my husband Rollie, who understands more about Civil War battle strategy than I ever will; of my daughter Katy, whose lifelong love of animals first inspired the idea for this book; and of my son Scott, whose support of my writing means more than he knows.

Finally, I would be remiss in omitting mention of a primary influence on the topic of this book--the bond between human and animal. I am grateful for the companionship of two dogs who sat faithfully by my side as I wrote--first, Hamlet, who died last year at age 19; and then, Oliver, the puppy who replaced him.

Marilyn Seguin
September 1997

WORKS CITED

Abel, Ernest L. "Faithful Friends." *Civil War Times Illustrated*, March/April 1995, pp. 46-52.

Adams, Richard. *Traveller*. NY: Alfred Knopf, 1988.

Bailey, Ronald H. *The Bloodiest Day: The Battle of Antietam*. Alexandria, VA: Time-Life Books, 1984.

Barrett, J.O. *The Soldier Bird Old Abe*. Madison, WI: Atwood & Culver, Publishers, 1876.

Barry, Joseph. *The Strange Story of Harper's Ferry*. Martinsburg, WV: Thompson Brothers, 1903.

Beller, Susan Provost. *Medical Practices in the Civil War*. Cincinnati: Betterway Books, 1992.

Biros, Florence W. *Dog Jack*. New Wilmington, PA: Sonrise Publications, 1981.

Boggs, S. S. *Eighteen Months a Prisoner Under the Rebel Flag*. Lovington, IL, 1887.

Botkin, B. A. *A Civil War Treasury of Tales, Legends and folklore*. NY: Random House, 1960.

Burnett, William G. *The Prison Camp at Andersonville*. Eastern National Park and Monument Association, 1995.

Coco, Gregory A. *On the Bloodstained Field*. Gettysburg, PA: Thomas Publications, 1987.

Colman, Penny. *Spies! Women in the Civil War*. Cincinnati: Betterway Books, 1992.

Copeland, Peter F. *From Antietam to Gettysburg: A Civil War Coloring Book*. NY: Dover Publications, Inc., 1983.

Dannett, Sylvia. *She Rode With the Generals: The True and Incredible Story of Sarah Emma Edmonds Seelye.* NY: T. Nelson, 1960.

Davis, Burke. *The Civil War: Strange and Fascinating Facts.* NY: Wings Books, 1960.

Dawson, William Forrest, editor. *Edwin Forbes' Civil War Etchings.* NY: Dover Publications, Inc., 1985.

Domestic Descendants. Time-Life Films Books, 1979.

Duncan, Russell, editor. *Blue Eyed Child of Fortune: The Civil War Letters of Colonel Robert Gould Shaw.* New York: Avon Books, 1992.

Edmonds, Sarah Emma. *The Female Spy of the Union Army.* Boston: Dewolfe, Fiske & Co., Publishers, 1864.

Finn, Peter. "Jackson's Horse Laid to Rest." *The Washington Post*, reprinted in Bangor Daily News, July 22, 1997, C1.

Forbes, Edwin. *An Artist's Story of the Great War.* NY: Fords, Howard and Hulbert, 1890.

Freeman, Douglas Southall. *R. E. Lee: A Biography*, vols. I-IV. NY: Charles Scribner's Sons, 1934.

Garrison, Webb. *Civil War Curiosities.* Nashville: Rutledge Hill Press, 1994.

Garrison, Webb. *A Treasury of Civil War Tales.* Nashville: Rutledge Hill Press, 1988.

Hawthorne, Frederick W. Gettysburg: *Stories of Men and Monuments as Told by Battlefield Guides.* Association of Licensed Battlefield Guides, 1988.

Jervey, Edward D., editor. *Prison Life Among the Rebels: Recollections of a Union Chaplain (Henry S. White).* Kent State University Press, 1990.

Larson, Rebecca D. *Roses of Intrigue.* Gettysburg, PA: Thomas Publications, 1993.

Leslie, Frank. *Frank Leslie's Illustrations: The American Soldier in the Civil War, A Pictorial History*. Stanley-Bradley Publishing Co., 1895.

Lewis, Thomas A. *The Guns of Cedar Creek*. NY: Harper & Row, Publishers, 1988.

Lippy, John D., Jr. *The War Dog: A True Story*. Harrisburg, PA: The Telegraph Press, 1962.

Magner, Blake A. *Traveller & Company, The Horses of Gettysburg*. Gettysburg: Farnsworth House Military Impressions, 1995.

Markle, Donald E. *Spies and Spymasters of the Civil War*. NY: Hippocrene Books, 1994.

McCutcheon, Marc. *The Writer's Guide to Everyday Life in the 1800s*. Cincinnati: Writer's Digest Books, 1993.

McLemore, Marcus S. *Civil War collector and owner of McLemore's Canine Training and Kennel*, Poland, Ohio. Personal interview, 20 May 1997.

Nesbitt, Mark. *More Ghosts of Gettysburg*. Gettysburg, PA: Thomas Publications, 1992.

Nevin, David. *Sherman's March: Atlanta to the Sea*. Alexandria, VA: Time-Life Books, 1986.

Newcome, Captain Louis. *Lincoln's Boy Spy*. NY: G. P. Putmans, 1929.

Nye, Col. W. S. "Jake Donelson, A 'Cocky' Rebel." *Civil War Times Illustrated*. March 1997, p. 28.

The Photographic History of the Civil War, vol. 5. Secaucus, NJ: The Blue and Grey Press, 1987.

Pratt, Fletcher. *The Civil War in Pictures*. NY: Garden City Books, 1955.

Rhodes, Robert Hunt, editor. *All For the Union: The Civil War Diary and Letters of Elisha Hunt Rhodes*. NY: Vantage Books, 1985.

Roberts, Nancy. *Civil War Ghost Stories and Legends*. University of South Carolina Press, 1992.

Robertson, James I. Jr. *The Civil War's Common Soldier*. Eastern National Park and Monument Association, 1994.

Robertson, James I., Jr. *Tenting Tonight: The Soldier's Life*. Alexandria, VA: Time-Life Books, 1984.

Scherich, Isaac W. *Army Service of Isaac W. Scherich*. Unpublished manuscript, not dated.

Silverstein, Alvin and Virginia. *Dogs: All About Them*. NY: Lothrop, Lee & Shepard Books, 1986.

Svenson, Peter. *Battlefield: Farming a Civil War Battleground*. NY: Ballantine Books, 1992.

Watkins, Sam R. Co. *Aytch: A Side Show of the Big Show*. Nashville, 1882. Reprinted by Broadfoot Publishing Co., 1994.

Wiley, Bell Irwin. *The Life of Billy Yank*. NY: Doubleday, 1971.

Wiley, Bell Irwin. *The Life of Johnny Reb*. NY: The Bobbs-Merrill Co., Inc., 1943.

Dispersion of the Army at Shreveport, LA, May 1865. (Frank Leslie's Illustrated)

INDEX

Abel, Ernest L. 148
Adams, Richard 148
alligator 134, 136
Andersonville Prison 108
Antietam (Sharpsburg) 119
Appomattox 5, 8, 58, 140
Arkansas 4, 10
Army of the Potomac 12, 30, 60, 66
Atlanta Cyclorama 91
Bailey, Ronald H. 148
Barry, Joseph 148
bear 10, 63, 111, 117
Belle Isle 32
Beller, Susan Provost 148
bird 6, 90, 93, 96, 125, 148
Biros, Florence 148
Boggs, S. S. 148
Botkin, B. A. 148
Burnett, William G. 148
Castle Thunder 6, 110-112
cat 10
Charlamayne 69
chicken 126
Cleveland, Ohio 22, 78
Coco, Gregory A. 148
Colman, Penny 148
Copeland, Peter F. 148
Dannett, Sylvia 149
Dart 45, 56
Daughters of the Confederacy 144
Davis, Burke 149
Dawson, William Forrest 149

DeMolay 128
Dick 54, 55
Don Juan 69
Duncan, Russell 149
Edmonds, Sarah Emma 149
Fanny 69
Farrar family 131
Fed 76, 125-127
Fido 5, 61
Fincastle Rifles 144
Finn, Peter 149
foraging 54, 85
Forbes, Edwin 149
Fort Hamilton 56
Fort Wagner 129
Fredericksburg 32, 138, 140, 147
Freeman, Douglas Southall 149
gander 11
Garrison, Webb 149
Gayoso Hospital 48
Geary 104
Gettysburg 4, 14, 24-26, 38, 56, 114, 115, 119, 138, 140, 146, 147-150
Giesboro 12
Grant 74, 85, 96, 105
Grey Eagle 69
Guillet brothers 122
Harper's Ferry 4, 20, 21, 148
Hawthorne, Frederick W. 149
Hero 6, 69, 74, 110, 112

hog 67

horse 5-7, 11, 12, 14, 54, 56, 60, 62-64, 66, 67, 69, 74, 77, 82, 83, 84, 97-99, 101, 103, 108, 115, 117, 118, 120, 122, 123, 128, 131, 138, 140, 141, 143-145, 149

Jack 4, 32-34, 62, 148

James River 55, 140

Jason 52

Jeff Davis 69

Jervey, Edward D. 149

Johnson's Island 147

Kelly's Ford 30

Kitty 6, 30, 100, 101

Larson, Rebecca D. 149

Leslie, Frank 150

Lewis, Thomas A. 150

Libby Prison 6, 81, 110-112

Little Sorrel 144

Longstreet 69, 104

Lucy Long 56, 69

Magner, Blake A. 150

Major 4, 27, 74, 122, 128, 129, 131, 146

Malvern Hill 32, 79

Mansfield, Ohio 146

Markle, Donald E. 150

McCutcheon, Marc 150

McLemore, Marcus S. 150

Mike 4, 30, 31

Miley 143

Minnesota 10

Mrs. M 50, 51

mule 5, 6, 9, 12, 53, 102-- 104, 106, 132

My Maryland 69

Nellie Gray 69

Nesbitt, Mark 150

Nevin, David 150

Newbern 117

Nye, Col. W. S. 150

Old Abe 6, 9, 90, 91, 148

Old Baldy 7, 69, 138, 139

Patterson 59

Pea Ridge, Ark. 19

pelican 10

Pennsylvania 11, 14, 24, 25, 32, 94

Petersburg 33, 64, 138, 140

pig 11, 48

Poland, Ohio 146, 150

Potomac 12, 30, 60, 66

Pratt, Fletcher 150

rabbit 79

rat 5, 7, 59, 66, 134, 135

Rebel 6, 7, 38, 96, 97, 107, 109, 110, 117, 124, 126, 148, 150

Rhodes, Robert Hunt 150

Richmond Howitzer Battalion 28

Rienzi 74

Rin Tin Tin 18

Roberts, Nancy 151

Robertson, James I. Jr. 151

rooster 7, 91, 96, 125, 126

Sabine Cross Roads 27

Salem Church 32

Sallie 4, 24-26, 146

Sam 62, 103, 119, 126, 127, 131, 134, 151

Savage's Station 32

Scherich, Isaac W. 151

sheep 54, 55, 88

Shiloh 10, 41, 103

Silverstein, Alvin and Virginia

151
Spec 56
Spot 6, 100, 107-109, 132
Spotsylvania 33, 140
squirrel 11
Staten Island 56
Sultana 136, 137
Svenson, Peter 151
Tige 100
Traveller 5, 7, 9, 56-58, 140-144, 148, 150
Turner 108, 111
Vicksburg 11, 90, 96, 134, 136
Virginia Military Institute 144
Washington and Lee University 141
Wauhatchie 104
Weldon Railroad 138
Western Reserve Historical Society 22, 39, 78, 146
Wilderness 33, 138, 140
Wiley, Bell Irwin 151
Wisconsin 9-11, 36, 90, 91